The Art of Coarse Acting

Michael Green

The Art of Coarse Acting

or

How to Wreck an Amateur Dramatic Society

Arrow Books

Arrow Books Limited
17-21 Conway Street, London, W1P 6JD

An imprint of the Hutchinson Publishing Group

London Melbourne Sydney Auckland
Johannesburg and agencies
throughout the world

First published by Hutchinson 1964
Arrow edition 1970
Reprinted 1975, 1976, 1980, 1984 and 1985

Printed and bound in Great Britain by
Anchor Brendon Limited, Tiptree, Essex.

ISBN 0 09 907530 X

I dedicate this book to:

Northampton Drama Club
Northampton Players
The Crescent Theatre, Birmingham
and the

Questors Theatre, Ealing

all of whom
(with the exception of Northampton Players)
survived me.

Acknowledgements

Although the Questors Theatre, Ealing, have tried to deny it, the author is very grateful to them for help with the illustrations.

Contents

List of Illustrations

Preface to the Revised Edition

As it is now some years since *Coarse Acting* was published I have taken the chance of another reprint to make some revisions and add new material. The way in which the book seems to have rung a bell with stage people – both amateur and professional – has been most gratifying and I was interested to find it is now recommended reading at some university drama departments. It is also a set book for a well-known London dramatic school bronze medal in speech and drama. I would have preferred gold but bronze will do. One of the most interesting developments has been the holding of Coarse Acting competitions in which various teams compete in displays of theatrical mayhem. The first was held at the Questors, Ealing, and the idea spread. The National Theatre entered a team in a contest to raise funds at Salisbury Playhouse and they were notable for a remarkable performance by the butler, who aged twenty years every time he entered the room, so he started off about thirty and ended up as ninety.

All this culminated in two shows based on the book. In 1977 I took *The Coarse Acting Show* to the Edinburgh Festival Fringe, with a company from the Questors, Ealing, and *Punch* was kind enough to describe it as the hit of the festival. Two years later, I put on a sequel at Edinburgh, *The Coarse Acting Show 2*, and this transferred to the Shaftesbury Theatre, London, the first (official) appearance of Coarse Acting in the West End. The 1977 show has been published by Samuel French as *Four Plays for Coarse Actors* and I can thoroughly recommend it. I need the money. *The Coarse Acting Show 2* is to be published by Samuel French shortly.

If I thought the original volume exhausted the subject, how wrong I was. I've received shoals of letters over the years detailing fresh stage horrors, such as the experience of the man who thrust at his enemy in a fight and rammed the sword through a scenery flat, where it wounded a passing ASM. A girl wrote to say she had wrecked the college *Pygmalion* by getting her parasol jammed in a crack in the stage, where it stuck so firmly they had to leave it for the rest of the play. Some students from Cambridge University told me they had founded a club for coarse lighting operators, The Shaft of Darkness Society.

My own experiences have broadened, too. When I wrote the original book I never dreamed that a few years later I would fall off the stage at a dress rehearsal, break a leg and be carried into a casualty ward dressed as an eighteenth-century smuggler. The nurse's surprise can be imagined when she discovered I had a wooden leg fixed to one knee and a knife sticking out of my chest. A parrot was sewn on my shoulder and my right arm terminated in a steel hook. There was a ghastly scar on my cheek. As a result my real injuries were ignored while the nurse tried to deal with the stage ones, tugging at the knife in my chest and trying to make the parrot fly away. Eventually she sent for the doctor, who said he'd make an appointment for me to have a better artificial leg fitted.

But enough. We have all suffered in the cause of drama, and the more true the story the more unbelievable the experience. I just hope this revised volume gives as much pleasure to we poor servants of the Muse as the original version appeared to do.

MICHAEL GREEN
Ealing, London 1979

Foreword

Why a foreword? Why indeed. Why must the show go on? Well, the show need not necessarily go on, as I have tried to show in succeeding pages, but the Foreword *is* going on, simply for the purpose of thanking all those who have ever acted with me for their part in some extraordinary experiences. One of the most enjoyable things about my sordid amateur acting career has been the friendships I have made, and I hope some of the friendships survive this book. Some, I am afraid, will not. While on the subject of the wonderful friendships one makes in the amateur theatre I should like to say that I publicly forgive the man in Birmingham who borrowed three pounds off me just before he went on stage and who was never seen again; and the person at Ealing who has got all my make-up, including the vital materials for Stock Character No. 3.

Perhaps I might also take the opportunity of appealing for the return of my complete Shakespeare, the coin which I used to twist in my tights, my braces and – but why go on? the list is endless.

MICHAEL GREEN

Prologue

(Preferably spoken by Mrs Bracegirdle)

Now doth the Muse of Drama stir this age
And thousands hear the lure of the stage.
Then see the truckling city clerk at night
Transformed into a royal and noble sight.
Bedecked in tinplate armour watch him tower,
A swelling monarch for his petty hour.
The spotty typist sheds her office weeds
And lo! We have a Carmen straight from Leeds!
Fear not. All amateurs are not the same,
Some Little Theatres higher standards claim,
And hold with fervour nigh obsessional
That amateurs are better than professional.
Yet amateur, profession'l, clown or Lear,
Someone must bear the message, grasp the spear.
With crêpe hair all askew, a parley hold,
Or tell the guests that dinner's getting cold.
It is for these poor servants of the Muse,
Coarse Actors all, that I this volume choose.
A dedication make, both brief and short
To those with cardboard spears at Agincourt.

1 An Introduction to Coarse Acting

'I had as lief the town-crier spoke my lines. . . .' HAMLET

What is a Coarse Actor? – the unhappiness with
Askew–the Unpleasantness at Birmingham–instant
Shakespeare – a clanger in Wagner

Many years ago I was in an amateur production of a play
with a friend called Askew. He is a man pathetically anxious
to do well on the amateur stage without any intention of
working to improve himself, of repulsive appearance and
totally lacking in the first principles of the business. He is one
of those people who whenever he walks on seems to be
wearing stilts inside his trousers. Together we have wrecked
many a carefully planned production.

In this play four of us had a whole scene in which we were
merely required to sit at the back of the stage and play cards,
occasionally making some interjection or other. One night, to
while away the time, we played a real game in which we
became completely immersed, while the main action continued
in front of us.

The only snag was that Askew had not bothered to learn
his lines but simply wrote them on the back of his playing
cards. This was fine until he played the card with his lines on
and I trumped it and shuffled it into the pack.

There was about fifteen seconds before the cue came.
Playing cards flew in all directions and half the pack went
under the table where Askew crawled on his hands and knees
looking for the vital card. The audience ignored the main
characters and concentrated on us, thinking something
desperate was about to happen under the card-table.

Eventually that cue came with three of us still under the table, there was a horrid pause and then with a cry of triumph Askew found his card and bellowed forth his two miserable lines from a kneeling position.

It was only afterwards he realized that he had found the wrong card and said the lines from the next act. However, nobody noticed the mistake and they all clapped like mad at the end of the scene.

That is Coarse Acting.

And what is a Coarse Actor or Actress? Those who are students of other coarse sports will know well enough. Those who are making their first acquaintance with this way of life may gain a clue from my definition of Coarse Rugby ('A game played by fewer than fifteen a side, at least half of whom should be totally unfit') and a Coarse Sailor ('One who in a crisis forgets nautical language and shouts "For God's sake turn left!"').

I would define a Coarse Actor as one who can remember the lines but not the order in which they come. It is, perhaps, not an entirely satisfactory definition, and a close friend whom I regard as easily the most desperately bad amateur actor in West Bromwich suggests that a Coarse Actor is one who can remember the pauses but not the lines.

However, that definition falls down because most Coarse amateurs don't have any pauses. They regard their lines rather as a machine-gunner regards a belt of ammunition: something to be shot off in the vague direction of the enemy and then replaced as rapidly as possible.

Other definitions which may prove accurate are:

One who knows when to come on-stage but not where

One who addresses the scenery instead of the audience

One who knows everyone else's lines better than their own (that is certainly true of Askew)

One who remembers the last play they were in better than the current one.

Certainly, one of the infallible signs that Coarse Drama is going on is the fact that the traditional roles of actor and audience are reversed. The actor is being himself while the audience are playing a part, heavily pretending to enjoy the show, struggling to laugh at unfunny jokes and so on.

Watching a bad amateur show can be more exhausting than three hours on stage.

Perhaps it all starts at school, where in a moustache made from burnt cork the trembling infant actor is pushed reluctantly on stage to mouth his halting lines while the child playing opposite bursts into tears for some unspecified reason. It is then that he discovers, execrable though he may be, that for the first time in his life several hundred people are actually paying attention to him.

It is too much for the immature mind. The false impression of those early days is confirmed as he grows older, until he really believes that his sixth-form performance of Aragon has made a major contribution to the drama, and that it did not matter about Portia's wig falling off or 'her' voice breaking halfway through rehearsals.

Indeed, schools drama forms a microcosm of the whole of Coarse Acting, thanks partly to the necessity for performing classical plays with large casts. It is true that in adult drama players do not run off stage sobbing because someone else has a nicer costume; nor are they, as younger children are known to be, sick on stage (and I write as one who in his first nativity play vomited over the Three Wise Men). But grown-up actresses are quite capable of refusing to play because they don't like their dress; and if Coarse Actors are not sick on stage they are often sick off stage, usually from sheer fright.

Naturally, most Coarse Actors are amateurs. A Coarse professional does not usually survive very long. But there are some Coarse Actors on the professional stage.

I once wrote the script for a television programme and the director cast an aged ham for a tiny part. It was a subtle part, of which I was rather proud. All he had to do was to spit. If I remember correctly, the dialogue went something like this:

ANNOUNCER: But there were those who said the whole voyage was useless.

Cut to c.u. of housewife.

HOUSEWIFE: Seems silly to me.

Cut to c.u. of businessman.

BUSINESSMAN: They'll never do it.

Cut to c.u. of old salt.

OLD SALT SPITS.

Good stuff, eh? Eventually we got to the telerecording and the director warned everyone that this was costing umpteen pounds a second, so we couldn't retake anything, so treat it as a performance boys and girls, and good luck, etc., etc. The cameras started and all went well until five minutes from the end, when they cut to the old salt. There was a thick silence for some five seconds (which cost the TV company about £10,000) and then he simply said, 'I'm terribly sorry, old boy, I've forgotten what you wanted me to do.'

I don't think he ever got another part. They did not ask me to write any more scripts.

Amateur acting is, however, littered with ex-professionals. It is never quite plain as to why they are ex. When asked why they quit the stage they usually have some fantastic yarn about having quarrelled with Binkie Beaumont over a major West End role.

I once acted with an old pro who had travelled all over the globe before the First World War. When he performed Shylock in Bulgaria the audience hissed. He thought he was going to be lynched until someone explained that hissing is a sign of approval over there.

This old dear had a sort of *droit de seigneur* on all our Shakespearean 'heavies'. The first time I met him was in *The Merchant of Venice*, in which he was Shylock, of course, and I was astonished at the first rehearsal when he started to make a series of moves that bore no relation to the director's plot. They also had no relation to the set, since one move consisted of tottering brokenly up a huge staircase, and we didn't have a staircase – he was supposed to go off left behind a flat.

The director, rather understandably, protested.

'Laddie,' came the reply, 'you can't teach an old dog new tricks. These moves were good enough for Sir Barry Jackson in 1924 and they ought to be good enough for you.'

But the amateur field remains the richest for the Coarse Actor. There are certain basic assumptions about a professional production – such as usually having a full cast – that rule out the best in Coarse drama. In fact it is one of the hallmarks of true amateur Coarse drama that, in the same way as Coarse Rugby or Cricket sides never have a full team, a Coarse play never has a full company.

I shall not easily forget a production of *Henry V* which coincided with an influenza epidemic. We were always one player short, in any case. It was a sort of floating gap, filled each night by whomever could get into the messenger's costume in time. If nobody achieved this then the stage manager bellowed something from the wings and the King edged his way across and held converse with an invisible man.

The epidemic, however, made things much worse. No one knew what part he would have to play next. Mysterious messages would be left at the office during the day ('Mr Green, someone rang to say you are Lord Scroop tonight. Does that make sense?').

Worse still, you would turn up at the theatre all unsuspecting, and be making-up as Bardolph or some such harmless role, when the stage manager would approach, thrust a heap of armour into your arms and say: 'Bert's ill. You're doubling the Earl of Essex tonight.'

Since there was no time to learn the appropriate lines, one came on stage, usually from the wrong side, groping about in ill-fitting armour and trying to read from the script at the same time.

It is hardly surprising that as a result I died after a sword fight which I should have won. Actually it was a little awkward because the other chap also died and we both tottered away clutching our vitals without having touched each other.

There was a nasty silence and the audience became restive. I managed to roll over and look at my script, which was pasted inside my shield, and saw I was supposed to make a speech over my opponent's bleeding corpse. Fortunately I had enough presence of mind to stagger to my feet in a manner which suggested I was merely winded and say a quick epitaph over my enemy (in view of the delay I cut the real speech and just muttered something about dust and a heap of bones).

The climax came when even with everyone doubling two or three parts there just weren't enough men to go round. The only thing left to do was to cut the play as we went along, omitting those on the sick list.

It was the quickest performance of *Henry V* on record. Whole episodes of English history vanished. The French court was reduced to one man. I don't think the Battle of Agincourt ever took place. In the end we discovered we had done it in five minutes over the hour, which as far as I know is a world record.

Yet however much Shakespeare suffers at the hands of Coarse Actors, they suffer for him too.

For me and many others a Shakespeare play is a mad whirl. I begin by rushing on stage and bellowing a line like 'My Lord, the French, with ill-advised speed do . . .' I am never allowed to go further because the King interrupts with an endless speech about what he's going to do to those Frogs, rebels, Scots, etc.

For the rest of the evening I rush through the dressingroom, changing beards and costumes every so often as I try to carry a spear for both sides, until finally, clad in insanitary and evil-smelling armour, I am spitted to death in the last battle, and die grovelling on a dusty floor with the hole in my tights exposed to the stalls.

Sometimes I die twice, or even three times. Coarse Actors are little better than sword-fodder.

As a treat, Coarse Actors are sometimes allowed to play Shakespearean clowns, or, more often, assistant clown. I need hardly say that Elizabethan comics are the unfunniest parts ever written. Just compare the hilarious lines Shakespeare gives to his serious characters ('Ah me, my uncle's spirit is in these stones, now heaven take my soul and England take my bones', as he writes in *King John*) with the stuff he dishes out to the comedians, erudite jests which sound like:

'By the Mass, ye are addle-pated as a coxcomb that hath lost his bells at Spitalfields, birlady and God's sonties, and if ye are not, let me be stuffed with a girt gurdy thugett and condemned to listen to a quondam thrasonical catch, aye marry fart and amen . . .'

Those lines are always spoken in a low growl, which

appears to be the stock clown's voice, and are accompanied by a funny walk and the placing of one's fingers on the forehead every so often. Fortunately the lines are so dreadful that it does not matter if one mixes them up or even forgets them entirely.

I once played the clown in John Marston's play *The Malcontent*, where I had the hilarious lines:

'He hath sore eyes . . . for the roots of the horns are in the eyeballs, which is why the horn of a cuckold is as tender as his eye.'

On at least half the performances I said, 'The roots of the eyeballs are in the horns', but far from spoiling the speech it usually got a laugh. I think it made as much sense as the original, at any rate. It is only fair to say the director did not agree.

Some day I should like to run a competition to find out the unfunniest clown in Shakespeare. There's a lot of choice, from that dreadful Launcelot Gobbo to the superlatively unfunny Feste. Nobody can make me believe that even the groundlings laughed at them, unless, as I suspect, the dire lines were enlivened by rude gestures.

Unfortunately, amateur directors are rarely honest about this. Professionals are more realistic. A former member of the Royal Shakespeare Company told me the most terrible moment of his career was when he received a letter asking him to play Touchstone. He immediately wrote back and asked if fifty per cent of the lines could be cut. Professional directors will take great pains over the clown scenes, making extensive use of amusing business. Amateur directors ignore the clowns but insist they are hilarious, against all the evidence of the script. As a last resort they may allege Shakespeare didn't intend the clown to be amusing, he meant him to be pathetic.

During a production of *Twelfth Night*, in which I had the misfortune to play Fabian, the director carefully explained that Feste was the elderly clown on his way out, which was why his jokes weren't funny, and Fabian was the up-and-coming clown. I pointed out that this theory broke down because Fabian was even more unfunny than Feste, but I could not convince him. I remember one line in particular:

'Sowter will cry out on'ı, though it be rank as a fox.'

Every time we came to that in rehearsal I said, 'Look, surely you don't really believe that's funny, do you?' and the director would assume an air of pitying superiority and say: 'It's actually extremely amusing to someone who understands it. Its simply the way you're saying it.'

I tried every way of saying that wretched line. I said, 'Sowter will *cry* out on it,' and I said, '*Sowter* will cry out on it,' and I said, 'Sowter will cry *out* on it,' and it still fell on the audience like a lump of suet pudding, until one evening I delivered it as usual and there was a great shout of laughter from the back of the hall.

For just a moment I thought I had triumphed over the Bard, when I realized that there was something familiar about the laughter. I glanced off stage and saw that the stage manager was not in his seat. He had collected every spare person, crept in at the back of the auditorium and organized a claque for the line. After that the real audience became convinced they were missing something and howled in all sorts of unexpected places. The only person who didn't think it hilarious was the director.

One is tempted to the theory that Shakespeare himself was a Coarse Actor. At any rate he was certainly experienced in Coarse Acting, as Hamlet's advice to the players shows: 'And let not those that play the clowns say more than is set down for them.' It seems to me quite obvious that Will Kemp and one or two others had got tired of those corny old jokes about sowter and horns and French tailors and started putting in some real gags. And after playing some of the clowns' parts I must say I don't blame them.

It is at this stage that I can imagine some people saying: 'That's all very well, but amateur standards have risen enormously in recent years. All this sort of thing doesn't happen now.'

The answer is that Coarse Theatre has its place even at the pinnacles of amateur drama. It was at the most famous Little Theatre in England that an actor in *King John* lost his way in a black-out at the end of a scene, fell off the edge of the stage and had to crawl up the aisle on his hands and knees before escaping through the emergency exit. Meanwhile, the stage manager decided to send out a search party drawn from members of the cast and the audience were surprised to find men in tights and carrying swords prowling round the aisles. One of them was even asked by an attendant if he wanted the toilet. Fortunately, many people were deceived by it all and one of them actually told the director it was a brilliant idea to use the auditorium as part of the acting area. 'It was total Theatre,' she said.

It was, by the way, at the same theatre that Osric waved his sword to start the famous duel in *Hamlet* and got it stuck in the proscenium arch. As a matter of fact I was the culprit and I felt a complete fool tugging away at my rapier while everyone cringed with embarrassment.

In fact the higher up the scale one goes, the greater the opportunities that seem to arise for a Coarse Actor, largely because in a bad production so much goes wrong that one thing more or less is not noticed, whereas in a carefully rehearsed piece any lone skullduggery stands out like a beacon.

My first experience of this was when I joined the famous Crescent Theatre (the Unpleasantness in Birmingham). My previous acting had been limited to small groups, so naturally I was anxious to do well, and was rather frightened of their reputation.

My first part was as a Russian peasant in *Wolves and Sheep* by Ostrovsky. I came on with the other peasants in the first scene and afterwards we changed into overalls and were used as scene-shifters. As we used to get in the way, smoking and chattering in the wings, the stage manager told us to clear out and go in the pub over the road until we were needed. We rather forgot about time over there until the First Peasant looked at his watch and said, 'We'd better hurry, there's only a minute to the change.'

We ran across the road and into the wings just as a burst of applause rang out. The First Peasant picked up a table and rushed on stage with it, while I followed with a potted fern.

At that moment I realized with horror that the curtain was still up. The applause had been for an actor's exit.

Fortunately I wasn't properly on stage. Only my overalled leg was visible, suspended in mid-air round a piece of scenery.

I slowly lowered the leg and gradually wormed it backwards out of sight.

The First Peasant wasn't so lucky. He did not realize his mistake until he was about to deposit the table on stage. It was then he became aware of a ghastly silence and a rustling in the audience. I must say, you couldn't blame the actors for stopping. It is rather upsetting when two men in overalls dash on in the middle of a scene and start heaving furniture about.

With great presence of mind the First Peasant put down the table, bowed and walked off stage with as much dignity as he could muster. There was one of *those* silences and then the scene dragged on.

After all that it was a pity that the peasant had put the table bang in front of a door so that one actor had to make a dramatic exit in his dressing-gown through the garden window.

Since then I have acted at other top-class amateur theatres and I have discovered that while they don't make so many mistakes as their lesser-known brethren, when they do make a blunder it's usually a mighty one.

No, Coarse Theatre still flourishes everywhere, from the humblest suburban hall to the greatest professional theatres in the land. It was at the Old Vic, no less, that I saw a Shakespeare death scene so ridiculous the audience laughed and someone cried 'encore'. I have even seen Coarse Theatre at The Royal Opera House, Covent Garden. At least, I don't think it was deliberate that Siegfried's sword broke and he had to go off and fetch another.

Never mind Siegfried. Nobody has ever paid me umpteen thousand pounds for a performance, but I know how you felt. And so do thousands of us.

2 A Coarse Actor's Approach to his Part

'Why do we feel embarrassed, impatient, ill-at-ease, assembled like amateur actors who have not been assigned their parts?'...'T.S.ELIOT *(The Family Reunion)*

Simple way of wrecking a play – no need to learn lines – the Unpleasantness in various places – what happened to Globovitch – 'Are you aware you are a Sodomite?'

Of all the people engaged in Coarse Drama the actor is by far the most important. The influence of the Coarse director or producer is small, and may even be completely negatived by a hostile cast. And while a Coarse stage manager may force his personality to the notice of the audience by setting the theatre alight, for instance (see Chapter 8), it is the actor who is chiefly responsible for ruining the play.

The smallness of the part has no relation to its wrecking possibilities. An actor has been known to kipper an entire production of *Macbeth* by running on and saying, 'The Queen, my lord, is *not* dead.'

In fact, a good way of whiling away time in a dressing-room is to have a competition to invent lines which would bring famous plays to a premature conclusion. An old pal always says his ambition is to wreck *Henry IV*, Part Two with, 'Falstaff, old fellow, you are very welcome to our Coronation'. Others which have won a bottle of beer are: 'Hamlet, I am no ghost, the poison missed my ear', and, 'The asp is dead'. The non-Shakespearean title is held by, 'Thank you, Professor Higgins, after one lesson I feel I can speak perfectly.'

What are the outstanding characteristics of a Coarse Actor? Firstly I should say a desperate desire to impress. The true Coarse Actor is most anxious to succeed. Of course, he is

25

hampered by an inability to act or to move, and a refusal to learn his lines, but no one is more despairing if he fails. In reality, though, Coarse Actors will never admit that they have done badly. Law One of Coarse Drama states: 'In retrospect all performances are a success.' In fact there is always someone who will maintain the show was better than the West End version.

No matter what dreadful disasters have occurred, a Coarse Actor will convince himself that all is well, and in this he is supported by kind friends who reassure him that he was splendid.

An acquaintance found himself quite literally trapped on stage. He couldn't find the way out (it was one of those rather complicated sets). So he simply forced a gap between two flats and squeezed off stage. But when I tackled him about it afterwards he merely said: 'Actually, old boy, you needn't worry. The audience didn't notice anything wrong. You merely *thought* there was something wrong because you knew the play'.

It is no use telling someone like that he was awful. 'The audience didn't notice a thing' is the hallmark of the Coarse Actor.

In common with many amateurs, a Coarse Actor firmly believes that the professionals have nothing to teach him. On the rare occasions on which he goes to the theatre he is quite capable of coming away and criticizing Sir Ralph Richardson for lack of inner sincerity, despite the fact that he moved hardened critics to tears. My friend Askew, for instance, always maintains that Laurence Olivier is not a great actor 'because he has cold eyes'.

'He doesn't *feel* it,' says Askew, who has never in his life remembered a line correctly.

One thing is certain: No Coarse Actor ever really improves, although occasionally he may become worse as his limited faculties desert him with age. All those training courses are wasted on a Coarse Actor. Train him for three years and at the end of it he will still walk on stage holding up his hands like a bunch of bananas.

There are, however, two main streams of Coarse Acting. There is the rather pathetic actor (or actress) who is desperately keen, utterly incompetent and very hard-working, the sort of person who spends six weeks rehearsing one line and forgets it on the first night. Askew's sister Maureen is like that.

And there is the actor who has some small ability, but is utterly lazy, the type who has one line and still carries a book around with him at the dress rehearsal. This section of actors and actresses are in the play simply for the drink and the company. A third group are both incompetent *and* lazy.

But in each case the result is the same. Watching two Coarse Actors perform together, one could not tell which had painstakingly rehearsed and which had not rehearsed at all. In fact, one would probably mistake the lazy actor for the hard-working one, because most lazy actors have a certain superficial competence which enables them to get through after a fashion whereas your diligent Coarse Actors are so obviously finding the whole thing a tremendous effort.

Everyone has experienced Coarse Acting. The finest players in the world have turned in coarse performances on occasions, or have been trapped in coarse productions. However, all can adjust themselves to their lot by adopting certain wheezes which I shall outline.

The first tip, or Primary Wheeze, is that in most plays people are cast not on their abilities but on their reputations. It is essential, therefore, to provide yourself with a ready-made reputation, as vague as possible ('Actually, I haven't done much since my Oxford Lear. The *Mail* was kind enough to find it definitive.'). Choose a story which gives you a let-out if challenged. 'Lear? Oh no, not Shakespeare's, it was a new play called *Leer* by a local author. Not Oxford University Dramatic Society, British Leyland actually. Yes, the Oxford *Mail* . . .' But since the amateur stage is the home of fantasy, there's little danger of being challenged, especially if you have the courage to make the lie a big one. The worst actor I have played with in my life claimed he used to act at the National Theatre.

One may well find getting a big part is less difficult than avoiding one. If you fear an important role would burst the bubble, decline gracefully, and hint you might just find time for something less demanding.

But make sure any small part accepted is not peculiar. I shall never forget entering a theatre for an experimental production and finding my best friend *chained to a pillar in the middle of the audience*. Apparently he was tied there half an hour before the play started and not released until the audience had left.

As he was supposed to be part of the play he could not even talk to his friends, but had to keep staring into space as they all kept asking what the matter was and offering him cigarettes. It was most embarrassing – we didn't know where to look.

Before rehearsals begin one must consider the characterization and the approach to the part.

A Coarse Actor will soon learn that in the same way as there are only a few basic jokes, so there are only a few basic parts, which for convenience I have numbered (see chart).

The first thing that will be noticed about the list is that there are no tragic old men or women on it. This is because all elderly people are funny on the Coarse stage.

HOW TO USE THE CHART: At first sight the chart would appear to be rather scanty, but in fact it contains all the few basic ingredients that are necessary.

On being cast, all an actor need do is ask the two vital questions: Am I old or young? And am I upper or lower class? Having decided (a spin of the coin is as good a way as any), he merely plays the basic part accordingly, remembering to add certain stock characteristics. For example, all clergymen are funny, all journalists are drunken, etc., etc. For the convenience of the keen student here is a list of some of the common characteristics:

Clergymen: half-witted, short-sighted.
Doctors: half-witted, short-sighted and absent-minded.
Army officers (elderly): bad-tempered, heavy drinkers, wear monocles.
Journalists: drunken, wear hats all the time indoors.
Policemen: tread like elephants. Do not know where to put helmet.
Authors: bearded and dirty.

ALL-PURPOSE COARSE-ACTING CHARACTER CHART

Stock character	Example	Make-up, etc.	Technique	Notes
1. Funny old man	Polonius	Long beard Mixture of lake, grey and midnight blue on face	Stoop Mow Gibber Squeak	Ear-trumpet?
1 (a). Funny old woman	Lady Bracknell	See above (beard optional)	As above	Wheelchair?
2. Funny young man (upper class)	Jack Worthing	5 and 9	Stammer. Utter vacuous laugh at intervals of ten seconds.	Monocle?
3. Member of working class (either sex)	Butler Maid Plumber	Should indicate stupidity	Adenoids. Drop h's and replace in wrong position. Occasionally say 'Oh ho'	Cannot fail to raise a laugh
4. General Coarse part	Messenger Third Citizen Bystander Sir Walter Blunt	Optional but vigorous	In Shakespeare, use standard Shakespearean voice, i.e. speak as if hailing a ship in a fog and sprinkle every other word with unnecessary syllables. Interject and grunt freely, whatever the part.	

Clerks: Twist hat in hand. Never stand upright before a superior.

Female cleaners: Arms akimbo. Cigarette dangles from lower lip.

An actor cast as a clergyman, for instance, first of all decides whether to play the part as an old man or a young man. Having decided to play his stock old man, he merely turns his collar the wrong way round and adds clerical idiocy and short-sightedness.

The list is rather old-fashioned, of course. But it is still valid because Coarse Actors don't base their performances on modern life or even the modern stage but on how they remember the part being played when they were young. In any case most plays of the Coarse Theatre belong to the past, so those old-fashioned police will be around for a long time.

However, Coarse Acting has infiltrated the realistic school. There is an all-purpose performance, played in old tennis shoes and jeans, which consists of grunting and jerking and adding 'like man' to every sentence. And the other standard types are still there, although now policemen tend to be corrupt and clever sadists, army officers corrupt and stupid sadists, journalists corrupt and moronic, and clergymen don't appear unless they have been unfrocked for a bestial offence. So old techniques can be adapted to new stereotypes.

Let me give an example from life of how this system can work out:

Askew put in for a production of *Hamlet* by an enthusiastic new director of a local society. After the reading we went into a pub on the corner and soon afterwards the director came in highly excited, went to Askew and said, 'I've got terrific news – I've cast you as Polonius.'

Askew took another swig of beer.

'Jolly good,' he said. 'Stock Character No. 1 I think will meet the case – funny old man. Do you mind if I give the same performance as for Justice Shallow? I rather liked that walk. I've got most of the make-up left as well. I don't suppose there's any chance of you cutting out that dreadful speech about "This, above all, to thine ownself be true" is there? I can't remember the lines these days.'

At this point I thought the director was going to burst into tears. Although it wouldn't have been the first time Askew had driven a director to hysteria. After being cast as the boatswain in *The Tempest* he asked, 'Do you want me to sew the parrot on the left or the right shoulder?'

Askew was quite serious. His idea of acting a sailor is to sew a parrot on his shoulder and cackle.

In the end Askew dropped out of *Hamlet* because the director insisted on his taking a curtain call, whereas he had counted on going off to the pub after being stabbed behind the arras. Askew has a list of parts which enable one to sneak away to the boozer, thanks to an early exit (Polonius, Lord Scroop, Constable of France, Doolittle, Prince of Aragon, etc., etc.).

Even more important is a black list of parts which will *not* let one get out for a drink. I don't mean merely the big parts, because a Coarse Actor will not normally secure those, but I also mean niggling little parts, such as Fortinbras, in *Hamlet*.

It is sad that so many directors these days will not co-operate with Coarse Actors in this sort of thing, and perhaps as important as a black list of parts is a black list of directors. I personally have an extensive one. Directors, of course, have their own black list on which I doubtless figure.

The sort to avoid is the young woman who directed me in some Russian epic. The lines were the usual Russian remarks, 'Shall I put some more logs on the stove?' and the part was plainly a sub-section of Stock Character No. 4 (all-purpose) with foreign overtones. A clear case for one rehearsal.

In fact I was not going to turn up until the night before the dress rehearsal, because there really is not much point in hanging around a draughty hall all evening simply for the privilege of saying 'Shall I put some more logs on the stove?' However, the director insisted that everyone attended all the rehearsals. We had to discuss our parts with her and she made us watch the scenes in which we weren't called so that we knew what it was all about. We even had to have discussions about what we had for breakfast and what the characters' parents were like.

Now a true Coarse Actor will not put up with this. I am proud to say that in ninety per cent of the plays in which I have performed I have never known what happened at either the end or the beginning. If I am not called early on I am in the bar until the curtain goes up, and if I've finished before the end I'm in the pub when the curtain falls.

And these weeks of endless rehearsal taught me nothing new. All the middle-class characters sat around saying lines like 'Five years since Uncle Petrovitch died', and then there would be a long pause and someone else would say 'Six', and after another long wait someone else would say 'And nothing has changed'.

They seemed to say the same lines in each scene, only by the time the last one was reached they all faced a grey, hopeless eternity. I'm glad I was in the cast – it must have been very depressing to pay money to watch it.

After three nights they actually got as far as my first entrance (of two). I was ready, winding myself up in the wings, but every time the cue came ('Ah, here comes Globovitch, our aged servant, who has been with us for fifty years') the director gave a childish wail and beat her tiny foot and squeaked, 'No, no, dear, you're not feeling that line.'

At this point a voice from the wings said, 'How much longer is that pretentious bitch going on like this?' and there was a further delay while the culprit was reprimanded.

Long past closing time I was still standing there waiting to go on when to my surprise they passed my cue without interruption. I immediately adopted Stock Walk No. 1(a), i.e. bending double, shaking my head, gnashing gums, mowing, gibbering meaninglessly, etc., etc. I jerked on stage and quavered, 'Shall I put some more logs on the stove?'

The familiar wail came from the darkness out front.

'No, no, Michael darling. You do see what's wrong, don't you?'

Well, I didn't, but I pretended to humour her and I said yes, and went out and did it again.

The reaction was even worse.

'No, Michael. Listen. You do understand there's a storm going on?'

'Yes.'

'There will be a howling of wind and the noise of rain on the roof.'

'Yes.'

'And an orchestra of serfs will be playing on the balcony.'

'Yes.'

'And you are a man who has been a friend of the family for fifty years, so you know that some of them are deaf.'

'Yes.'

'So you do see what I'm getting at, don't you?'

'No.'

I hoped she would have a fit, but after breathing heavily for a moment she simply shrieked, 'I want you to bloody well speak louder.'

The outburst did little good because I went into a deep sulk and boomed my lines so loudly for the rest of rehearsal that the leading lady said I had given her a headache.

A true Coarse Actor will always be on guard against the efforts of directors like that to read too much into his tiny part, although she was not as bad as the one who said loudly during rehearsals for some rather deep piece of drama: 'Michael, dear boy, you do realize you are supposed to be a sodomite, don't you?'

It is best to deal with your director even before the first rehearsal. The simplest way is to arrive for the reading with a phoney domestic crisis that can be activated whenever necessary ('I should like to play, but you do know that my wife's ill, don't you? It might mean missing one or two rehearsals').

Ill-health is an excellent excuse because it gives one a chance to play for sympathy and to enlist the natural hostility of any cast towards its director ('He actually forced Fred to come to an extra rehearsal when the poor chap hasn't been well for months. He's just a swine. I'll never be in one of his shows again').

For the record I shall formulate all this as the Second Wheeze of Coarse Acting: 'Upon being cast, a Coarse Actor immediately suffers from illness and domestic or business crisis.'

At some stage of the rehearsal period a Coarse Actor will be expected to know his lines. Since learning them is out of the question, one should devote the early rehearsal time which is often wasted by the director in improvisations or discussing motivation to adopting simple methods of having a crib available. I have already recounted the story of the man who wrote his lines on playing cards. Starched cuffs are another good repository and in emergency the part can be written on the wrist with a ball-point pen. In costume drama I have known lines written on the blade of a cardboard spear, and a toga will conceal a complete script in its capacious folds. One may also chalk them on the inside of one's shield and even paste a page of the script there. Askew often keeps a crib inside a cigarette case, which can be produced in times of stress.

But try to learn the technique of merely glancing at the lines surreptitiously. It looks rather odd if a messenger addresses his speech to the end of his own spear, instead of to the King. In the incident to which I am referring some of the King's lines were, by arrangement, also on the end of the same spear, and the two of them fought over it, sawing backwards and forwards between them in a most untheatrical fashion.

A useful device in connection with lines is Askew's Sneer Chart. This is simply a script marked not only with moves but with every emotion and facial expression he may be called upon to register. Thus a simple line like: 'You unutterable swine – you'll suffer for this' is marked as follows: 'You (*breathe heavily twice*) unutterable swine (*snarl and march downstage*) – you'll (*pause five seconds*) suffer for this' (*raise right arm to 45 degrees, assume expression no. 6 and hold till curtain*).

It is also wise, during the rehearsal period, to copy out any letters, scrolls, etc., one has to read. It is rather alarming to rely on reading a letter and to pull out a blank sheet of paper from the envelope.

And so the scene is set for the first night. After attending the minimum of rehearsals, you are safe in your stock characterization, and all arrangements have been made about lines. More important still, you know things about what is going to happen on stage that the director does not know. I shall describe these in the next chapter.

3   A Coarse Actor Prepares

'Nor do not saw the air too much with your hand, thus . . .'
(Hamlet)

How to be conspicuous—conceal intentions from director—
the actor who exploded – more Unpleasantness – when
Lady Macbeth put her foot in it – the uneasiness of Cardinal
Pandulph

Let us assume that a Coarse Actor has survived the difficult
rehearsal period. The first night of his play has now arrived.
What is a Coarse Actor's first thought? Surely it is: HOW CAN I
MAKE MYSELF CONSPICIOUS?

Now in fact that is *every* actor's thought, the serious ones as
well as the Coarse variety, but those who obtain large parts
don't have to go out of their way to do it. Only the Coarse
Actor, thrust to the back of a spear-wielding mob, or reduced
to carrying in a tray full of drinks, has to invent stratagems
and ways and means of ensuring that his friends and relatives
in the audience can register his effectiveness.

In this connection it is worth quoting the experience of a
friend who was playing one of a huge crowd of Russian
citizens in a play about the Revolution. It was his first part
with the company, and my friend spent hours on a careful
make-up and invited all his family only to find the crowd was
so dense and the stage so small, he couldn't get on stage.
'There were about ten of us fighting in the wings to get on,' he
recalls. 'I never got nearer than the stage manager's desk.' A
warning of the dangers of being too modest.

It is therefore necessary to forget the nonsense that is
usually written about acting being teamwork, pulling together, sinking your identity, etc., etc.

What is really meant by teamwork is that everyone pays court to the main players. If you doubt the truth of that statement just try to make up in the leading lady's mirror.

No, an amateur dramatic performance is not teamwork, it is a free-for-all between a dozen egos, and the ego which gets there firstest with the mostest will win.

But how, comes the question, can I get there firstest with the mostest when I have only three lines at the back of the crowd?

Well, there are certain wheezes which will achieve the desired end, and other little hints which can at least ensure that you go through the show with the minimum of inconvenience. The first is MAKE-UP.

One will, of course, be using one of the stock make-ups described in the chart on page 29. However, there is no reason why these should not be improved upon.

Askew's cousin Watkins had merely to walk across the stage as a bystander in a street scene. When he went on there was such a gasp from the audience that I thought he must have made a rude sign at the stalls (not even a Coarse Actor would stoop as low as that for effect, although I have known a harassed professional do it).

When I peered from the wings I saw why he had caused such a sensation. He had put real character into the part. To start with he had strapped one leg up and was walking with a crutch. He wore dark glasses and carried a placard – 'Blind'. He had put on a false nose so revolting that one could not describe it. Boils were plastered all over his face and there was a great bruise on his forehead which looked like a third eye. No one could miss him.

Directors do not take kindly to this sort of thing, so it cannot be too strongly emphasized that no hint must be given before the first night. Many a promising Coarse Actor has had his tricks frustrated because he was foolish enough to introduce them at the dress rehearsal. The golden rule at the dress rehearsal is simply to lie low and go through the normal business with a subdued make-up. In Watkins's case he had walked across the stage normally at the dress rehearsal and then smuggled in his crutches secretly on the first night.

The director, by the way, kicked up an awful fuss and took

away his crutches, so next night Watkins was towed in on a little trolley like Porgy in the Gershwin musical. For some reason we never saw the director again after that, but he still writes to us from Canada.

Perhaps the example I have quoted is rather a bold one, but there is certainly no reason why a Coarse Actor should not use every cosmetic aid he can find in his own or someone else's make-up box.

Incidentally, don't waste money buying your own make-up. If there are several Coarse Actors in a show it is much the best if they all buy one stick and then pool the result. But just make sure everyone does not buy the same stick.

As a comparatively young actor I had a part in *King John* as Second Citizen of Angiers. I was carefully sorting out various sticks of make-up when I noticed that the First Citizen had mixed together a foetid sort of mud-pie of lake, Nos. 8, 21, 4, and 2½, and was plastering it all over his face.

'I believe in experiment,' he said thickly through the cake which covered his features. 'After all, I reckon you've got to be pretty old to become First Citizen of an important place like Angiers.'

The effect of this apparition rising over the battlements of the beleagured city would have struck fear into the stoutest heart. King John visibly quailed, while the Duke of Austria burst into laughter (although this was partly due to his having drunk three bottles of Guinness before he went on). It was a lesson I never forgot. In Coarse Acting there is no compromise. One is young or senile, fit or crippled. The younger an actor is, the older and more decrepit he tries to be. I have seen school shows with entire armies of limping men.

However, be careful of the man with the home-made substitute for cosmetics, the sort of person who says: 'You don't want to use that expensive removal cream, old boy, why don't you go to the ironmonger's and get a tin of lawn-mower grease? It's just as good and much cheaper.'

After your face has burst into flames you will return to removal cream.

Beware of too many artificial make-up aids. A man in a bank society was so determined on an outstanding make-up that he not only put on a false nose of putty but inserted rubber tubing inside his mouth to distend the lips, padded the inside of his cheeks with cotton wool, pinned back his ears with sticky tape and to cap it all wore a false beard, moustache and a wig.

He took the ideas from some book on acting, one of those volumes that forgets you might have to speak with all that lot on the face.

Halfway through his first speech he sneezed. The effect was alarming. He simply exploded in a cloud of make-up. Cotton wool and rubber tubing shot from his mouth, his nose whizzed across the stage and every piece of false hair fell off. His ears came unstuck with a pinging sound and I believe one of his warts landed in the stalls.

When the dust settled a totally different person was standing there. It was the best transformation scene I have ever witnessed.

PREPARATION. Presuming that all is well with your make-up, and your mind is firmly settled on the stock characterization, there will be nothing to do except wait for the call, provided you have been lucky enough to reach the theatre in time to have a few minutes to spare. This breathing space should be turned to advantage.

Not that I hold with the school of thought which says that an actor should put himself through a series of relaxing exercises before taking the stage – a sort of yoga performance. I saw a young American do this. He lay down on three chairs in the dressing-room and began breathing deeply. First he raised one arm and then the other, and then one leg and then the other, until all four limbs were off the ground, and then he let them all fall with a thump. At the same time he exhaled with a ghastly hiss, like when a football is punctured. He was so wrapped up that he missed his cue.

Personally I find a quart of light ale is wonderfully relaxing for the vocal chords, and takes one's mind off the play. But there are obvious risks involved in drinking large quantities before going on. Many an actor has had to make a hurried and unscripted exit because of this.

And please remember that in costume plays once you're in

your tights and armour you're *in*. We do not want such
incidents as when the Constable of France urgently whispered
to me, 'I can't wait any longer, just say my line for me, will
you, old man?' and rushed off stage. This was particularly
difficult, because I was supposed to be dead by the time his
line arrived.

This is especially embarrassing if you have to share a toilet
with the public (as in the old Questors Theatre, Ealing). I
shall never forget the look on the face of one of the audience
when I rushed into the gents, hurled my spear and shield into
a corner, and tore down my knitted chain-mail. I had an
arrow sticking out of my back ready for the next scene and he
kept staring at it.

A Coarse Actor is perfectly entitled to ignore any director
who objects to drinking in the dressing-room. Perhaps I may
be allowed to quote the exact dialogue which took place
between myself and a new director a few years back.

DIRECTOR: (*entering dressing-room*): Michael, is that beer you're
drinking?
ME: Yes, do you want some?
DIRECTOR: You'd better put it away at once. It won't improve
your performance you know.
ME: —————.

   (*Exit outraged new director.*)

I flatter myself that Coward could not have bettered the
terseness of that dialogue.

But strong drink should not be taken on stage. The last
time I saw this rule broken a fountain of light ale sprayed
from the flies on to the actors below. It came from the god in
Giraudoux's *Amphitryon 38*. Finding the heat and the boredom
intolerable as he waited in the flies to be lowered on a
cardboard cloud, he stored some beer inside the cloud and
helped himself whenever he felt inclined, which was pretty
often. When it became clear that bottled beer shot forth
as foam at that temperature he tried a small flask of brandy,
with the result that on the last night the cloud was lowered
and no god appeared. Someone peered inside and found him
asleep.

A little flirting with the female members of the cast and stage team will help to relax the nerves, but avoid anything in the nature of an orgy. Save that for the last-night party.

Do not fill in time in the dressing-room by playing chess. Inevitably the game will spread on to the stage. I think it was in *Henry IV* Part One that I played with a fanatic who used to whisper to me on stage, 'Have just moved Knight to QB3 and taken your rook.' This worried me so much that after addressing the King as 'My Pawn' I forgot to charge off-stage with the others. Eventually we formed a chess league among the royal army, until the background to every scene was a heaving mass of actors muttering chess moves to each other, and the game was banned in favour of cribbage.

Smoke by all means, but please do not stub out the unfinished cigarette and then put it behind your ear. It distracts the audience and in any case might be lost.*

Personally, I make a habit of carefully handing my lighted cigarette to the stage manager just before I walk on. If he refuses to accept it I am always most careful to stub it out on the back of a flat. It is these little disciplines that distinguish a real man of the Theatre.

But take care to expel the smoke before going on-stage. Askew's sister Maureen ruined part of *HMS Pinafore* by taking a big puff in the wings, just as she entered. When she sang her first note smoke poured from her mouth and nostrils and obliterated her.

Look out for crêpe hair. It will sizzle away merrily if hot ash drops on it and may even burst into flames.

Care should also be taken in what one eats before a performance.

It is unpleasant to play a love scene with someone who has just eaten garlic cheese sandwiches. This happened to Watkins, who up to then had quite enjoyed the scene, so much so that the director had to restrain him in rehearsal.

He was supposed to be positively squeaking with desire for this woman. In fact he was saying that if she wouldn't let him sleep with her he would shoot himself. The effect was rather spoiled because there was an expression of utter revulsion on

* The practice of stubbing out a cigarette on a cardboard shield is highly dangerous.

his face as he spoke his impassioned words. When it came to the final clinch he couldn't face her, and just pecked the side of her neck.

Diet can cause other hazards, too. I remember a village performance of a play in which a sick member of an expedition decides to shoot himself to avoid being a burden to the others. When the other explorers had left the stage ('God, but the insects are terrible, Fanshaw') he painfully crawled from his sleeping-bag to the tent pole and reached up for his revolver, which hung there. Unfortunately, as he grasped the fatal weapon he loudly broke wind. This rather spoiled the dramatic effect of his death, especially as someone in the stalls whispered, 'When the stage directions said he shot himself there must have been a misprint . . .'

The moment before taking the stage is a particularly nerve-racking time. The best way of spending the last few moments is to make a check on costume and hand props.

A simple routine might go like this:
> Trousers – are they done up?
> Cigarette case?
> Shoes – have you got them on?
> Sword? (Ah, ha, you lent it to the French Herald, didn't you? And he's on stage with it, isn't he? What are you going to do now, mate?)
> Do you know where the prompt is?
> Is the pistol loaded?
> Have you got the letter? (And make sure it is not the one the stage manager gave you, but your own copy with the lines written inside.)
> Do you know your way around the stage? (Not such a silly question. I have seen Lady Macbeth come magnificently down a staircase, only to put her foot in a brazier at the bottom.)
> Do the doors open inwards or outwards?
> Have you taken off your cycle clips?
> Has anyone played a practical joke?

The last item is most important. Those who are not experienced actors may think it unnecessary, but any Coarse

Actor worth his salt will agree it is vital. I shall not forget the occasion when an actor's cloak was nailed to the floor as he stood waiting in the wings, lost to everything except his part.

The man was playing Cardinal Pandulph in *King John* and the whole affair was especially interesting, because the Cardinal's entrance followed what is one of Shakespeare's worst lines: 'Here comes the Holy Legate of the Pope.'

Well, the Holy Legate strode on firmly, came to a sudden halt, clutched his neck with a strangled cry and vanished into the wings. The audience thought it was a brilliant piece of character acting.

Meanwhile, off stage there was the sound of swearing and quarrelling and noise of a cloak being torn free from nails. Finally the Cardinal appeared again to the accompaniment of rending cloth, and immediately forgot his first line.

Do not spend the waiting time necking in the wings with actresses or stage staff. Amateur musical societies are particularly prone to this, and I recall a performance of *Lock Up Your Daughters* where I missed an entrance because I was writhing behind a flat with pretty young ASM. To make it worse, she went off with someone else at the last-night party. If you want to seduce someone during the show, choose a scene in which you are not called.

All the foregoing instructions having been carried out, a Coarse Actor is now ready to make his or her entrance upon the stage. In the next chapter I shall describe how to make the best of yourself when you get there.

4 A Coarse Actor Performs

'On the stage he was natural, simple, affecting, 'twas only that, when he was off, he was acting.' GOLDSMITH

Remarkable interpretation of Ghost in *Hamlet* – critics dumbfounded – how to steal a scene without saying a word – standing out in a crowd – more Unpleasantness – some simple wheezes

A Coarse Actor's performance problems begin *before* his entrance. How often has one watched an amateur show and stared fascinated at the bulging curtains, or the wobbling scenery, which mark where a Coarse Actor is trying to grope his way on stage. For a successful performance, therefore, make sure of the entrances. Check that the stage management have not nailed up the door or pinned together the curtains. They seem to have a compulsion to do that sort of thing.

Do not worry if the entrance goes wrong. Coarse Actors are most vulnerable at this point. It is at the entrance that Green's Syndrome is liable to strike. This is a desperate feeling of panic and unreality as you march into the lights. It all seems so unreal – the lights, the heat, the people. I keep asking 'What am I doing here?' It is then I wish I had either had that extra gin or not had it, as the case may be.

Some actors trip up over anything within six feet. Short-sighted players, not allowed to wear their glasses, may blink owlishly all over the stage before fixing a glassy stare on the person to whom they are supposed to be speaking, unless, as often happens, they address the wrong character.

This sort of thing is less important than appearing at the wrong time – possibly in the wrong scene or even in the wrong play, as happened to Askew at a one-act festival. Don't close the door until you are absolutely sure the entrance has been made at the right point. If the cast pay no attention to you or break off abruptly in the middle of conversation it may be wiser to go out.

Make sure the cast are dressed in the same period as yourself. Askew's blunder was particularly bad because the scene was the bar of a golf club and suddenly Askew marched in dressed as Julius Caesar.

Naturally, a bad entrance is rather distressing after one's appearance has been built up in preceding scenes, but fortunately Coarse Actors are not likely to have a part which is big enough for that.

A possible exception is in an amateur musical, where Coarse Actors may find themselves with a 'funny' non-singing part, the entrance to which is heavily telegraphed by lines like these (to be said in a strangulated tenor voice):

Ah, here comes Rudolpho, our comic servant. He is a risible fellow and will amuse us for a moment or so. But soft, I will play a jest upon him. He will be drunk, and if I put on the Burgomaster's hat he will think that I am the old Burgher himself, ha, ha, ha.

ALL: Ha, ha, ha.
SONG: 'The Burgomaster's Hat.'

However, since it would defy Chaplin himself to raise a laugh after a build-up like that, it won't matter if the entrance goes wrong.

While it is depressing to come on stage when the situation calls for a roar of laughter, and to be received in silence, the Coarse Actor who has read this book will at least be prepared for the silence. He will not be left stranded in the doorway waiting for the non-existent mirth to die down.

It is much worse to come on as a serious character and to be received with a howl of delighted amusement, although it is gratifying to know one has been noticed. I can claim to be one of the few actors who has raised a laugh on entering as the Ghost in *Hamlet*.

The director was a little worried about my interpretation in rehearsal. He kept saying, 'Michael dear, I don't think the Ghost would walk with both arms held out in front of him and wailing like that.' And he absolutely forbade me to rattle some chains as I walked.

I cut the wailing and the chains, but I secretly rehearsed what I thought would be a most effective piece of business and put it into operation on the first night, as recommended in the preceding chapter.

When the cue came ('See where it comes again') I stuck my hand, in a clutching attitude, round the edge of the scenery, and sawed it up and down a little. By a happy coincidence the lighting threw a shadow of my hand on the backcloth.

There could be no doubt as to the effectiveness of this, because half the audience collapsed in hysterics, before I even got on stage. I believe the director collapsed, too, although I have never found out his real reactions, as he has not spoken to me since.

However, the local paper were most impressed.

'As the Ghost,' wrote their critic, 'Michael Green blew away the dust of tradition that says the apparition should be a dull, self-pitying shade, and made him a real character, full of wit, fun and sly humour, a man Hamlet would indeed have admired and wanted to avenge.'

So out of evil came good.

All this presumes one is entering alone, but it is the lot of Coarse Actors frequently to enter in a crowd. There is a simple rule to make yourself noticed in a crowd entrance and that is *to come in late* (the Tertiary Wheeze). The inexperienced player will try to force his way to the front of the queue in the wings, but the old hand will merely stand back, finish his cigarette quietly and then calmly stroll on stage about one and two-fifths seconds after the rest. It is a trick that never fails.

Incidentally, members of the chorus of amateur musicals might like to try the experiment of finishing a song a note after everyone else. It is equally effective.

Once the entrance has been made, one's duty is clear:
TO SHINE.

Remember that as a Coarse Actor you are fighting the hostility of the author, who gave the part only four lines, and bad ones at that; the director, who wants to hide you; and the rest of the cast, who have their own problems. So it will be a struggle, but a rewarding one, to impose your own personality.

You will already, of course, have found out from the seating plan the position of friends and relatives, or alternatively the critic of the local paper. Firstly, then, no matter to whom you are supposed to be speaking, swivel round and address lines directly to these seats.

The effect on them will be quite remarkable, and the effect on the play will be no worse than if you were speaking to the other actors.

In this connection one must protest at the increasing tendency to produce plays in the round. Apart from the fact that far from being experimental it is very old hat, it is sheer death for the Coarse Actor. How can one deliver lines to a particular section of the audience when some of them may be sitting behind and some in front? I did know an actor who managed it by making his big speech while marching round the perimeter of the acting area, and another who achieved some success by standing in the middle and slowly revolving on the spot as he spoke, only he became tangled up in a telephone wire towards the end.

The round brings other problems too. What can the heroine of a classical play do if every time she sits down her dress gapes open at the back, exposing the marks of her bikini?

Now this sort of thing is expected in every Coarse production, but on a picture-frame stage it doesn't matter. If wardrobe have provided an actress with a gaping dress then she just makes sure she faces the front all the time. But acting in the round gives no chance to amend little costume faults. An actor who comes on-stage with his trousers unzipped will have no chance to kneel behind the sofa and repair the omission in private.

There is an endless strain on the actor, even down to the last detail. In small theatres the audience can even read anything that is written. My friend Askew had a habit of doodling vulgar words when he had to write anything on stage and was horrified to hear the voice of a child on the front row spelling one of them out as he was taking a telephone message.

But to return to the Coarse Actor's problems. I have said that the first duty of every Coarse Actor is to project himself and I would draw the attention of earnest students to the picture, which is a classic example of how to steal a scene even without having any words to say.

The photograph was taken during a performance of my production of *Bulldog Drummond* ('I have seldom been less in sympathy with a production,' wrote the critic of that well-known literary journal the *Middlesex County Times*).

The situation is as follows: Drummond (foreground, in plus-fours) has been bound hand and foot and tied to a chair. His girl friend Phyllis has been doped and placed in the next chair. Dr Lakington (a sadistic German scientist, in white coat) has ordered some champagne to drink a toast before raping the girl. The champagne is brought by a Chinese mute (don't ask me why). After he brings it Dr L. orders him from the room.

Now here is a little test. Given that situation, which actor should be able to dominate the scene?

The answer at first sight would appear to be the Chinese mute. Fantastics always steal the scene, as do children and animals. When they are mute and carrying a champagne bottle it is too easy. Drummond and Phyllis, unconscious, appear to be out of the fight.

In this production the mute made every effort to live up to the opportunity, although he was up against some severe competition from Dr Lakington, who wrote in a lot of his own lines such as '*Donner und Blitzen*' and 'Chinese scum'. But the mute simply grinned and winked and made vague yammering noises. He seemed a certain winner. *Yet Drummond stole the scene*.

The picture explains why. With masterly presence of mind, just as the mute was about to make his funny face, Drummond regained consciousness and started to writhe wildly in his chair, voiding himself of dreadful moaning noises. The audience immediately switched their attention to him, and the mute's efforts went for nothing.

Note that Drummond had the presence of mind to save all this for the first night. There was no hint of it in rehearsal, so there was no opportunity for me to cut the business (which I most certainly would have done). I do not approve of anyone getting a laugh in my productions unless I have the credit.

What a perfect example of Coarse Acting! Isn't it a lesson to us all in swift thinking and artistic integrity? Study Drummond's writhing figure and contorted features again and ask: Could I measure down to that standard of acting?

Incidentally the picture shows that of the four actors on stage, one is not really trying. I am afraid the girl who played Phyllis, although a dear, sweet little thing, was just not bad enough to make a real Coarse Actress.

Unfortunately opportunities of the sort which occurred in *Bulldog Drummond* are rare, because Coarse Actors are so often lost in a mob.

It is possible, however, for a skilled actor to stand out even in a crowd, despite the handicap of having no lines. Here is another example, this time from a production of *Julius Caesar*.

Watkins was in the crowd, playing nothing particular, just one of the rude mechanicals – Sixth Citizen, I think. He was not considered good enough to have any lines, not even gems like 'O woeful day' which the first, second, third, fourth and fifth citizens were spouting.

Yet he overcame this handicap in an extraordinarily simple manner. During Mark Antony's speech over the body of Ceasar he carefully placed himself centre stage and simply repeated every other line that Mark Antony said.

The scene eventually went something like this:

MARK ANTONY: Friends, Romans and countrymen, lend me your ears. . .

SIXTH CITIZEN: Ah, ears, ears, ears (*nodding and grimacing to the other citizens*).

MARK ANTONY: I come to bury Caesar, not to praise him.

SIXTH CITIZEN: Ah yes, praise him, praise him. Ah, praise him.

MARK ANTONY: The evil that men do lives after them. The good is oft interrèd with their bones.

SIXTH CITIZEN: Ah, bones, bones. Interrèd with their bones.

Not content with that, as the speech went on he added gestures. So when Antony came to the lines: 'Here is the will and under Caesar's seal to every Roman citizen he gives to every several man seventy-five drachmas', Watkins danced for joy and began to count imaginary drachmas.

There were undoubtedly members of the audience who never so much as looked at Mark Antony during that speech. In fact some probably thought Watkins was Mark Antony.

His success went to his head and he tried the same business in *Henry V*. During Henry's speech to the citizens of Harfleur in which he threatens them with 'your naked babies spitted upon pikes' the audience were astonished to see a pike arise from the back of the English army and make savage spitting motions. In this case, however, Watkins overstepped the mark because Henry V, who had been a noted rugby player in his youth, personally threatened him with violence if he ever did it again.

In fairness to Watkins he was only adopting a technique much loved by the professional theatre, where the standard crowd noise is to repeat the last line of what the main character has said. One can hardly blame a mere amateur for copying the device.

In addition to the above, crowd members are traditionally licensed to write in vague noises of their own invention, grunts such as Urgh, Aaah and Yurch, plus the inevitable Hooray-ray-ray all-purpose coarse cheering sound. At the end of any rousing speech a crowd may gain extra lines by announcing what they intend to do. Examples are: 'To the Bastille!'; 'Death to the traitors!'; 'To the breach, to the breach!'; 'On towards Dunsinane!'; 'Arrest Peer Gynt!' etc., etc. So as to make no mistake, Askew actually prepares his own script for crowd scenes, a sheet of paper covered in ejaculations and grunts. He also believes the traditional crowd noises of 'rhubarb' should be in period. Thus in *Julius Caesar* he was distinctly heard to mutter 'Rhubarbum, rhubarbum . . .'

Those who wish to delve further into the subject can do no better than to listen to BBC radio plays and dramatized documentaries, especially the schools programme and Radio Four. Here may be heard many examples of Coarse acting in crowds.

But even among Coarse crowds there is a code. If anyone

tries to hog the scene too much, the others are perfectly entitled to sabotage his efforts. The best way of doing this is for everyone to gang up on the offenders and stand in front of them. They cannot do much behind a wall of living flesh.

TECHNIQUE. The amount of genuine acting which a Coarse player will be called upon to do is limited. To start with he will merely be called upon to register certain simple emotions. The only emotions that need be used are as follows:

1.	RAGE	4.	JOY
2.	PLEASURE	5.	PAIN
3.	LOVE	6.	HATE

And even in this simple list the same expression may serve for two emotions (see pictures). Once an actor is able to register these stock emotions successfully he can introduce subtleties if he wishes by mixing two emotions.

For instance, to portray a man who although badly injured has succeeded in saving his fiancée from death, one merely mixes emotions 3, 4 and 5. To portray a man like Othello, furious with the object of his devotion, is simply a matter of mixing emotions 1, 3 and 6.

Have no truck with any director who requires impossible subtleties of feeling. If he says 'I want you to give me that underlying sense of insecurity' simply hand him the list and ask him to tick off the required emotion.

STAGE FIGHTS. All sword fights on the Coarse stage are conducted on the same principle, namely that both contestants aim a series of meaningless blows at each other's weapons (see picture) and never at each other. Sometimes this is done to a pattern: clash swords at shoulder level, clash at knee height, clash again at shoulder level in a figure-eight motion. Usually one swordsman is out of time and the other has to wait for him. A simpler version is for one man simply to hold up his sword and for the antagonist to beat at it savagely. The important thing is that no stroke should be aimed at an opponent, only at his sword or his shield, and only then if he has several seconds' warning, which is usually given by a ten-second backswing. While a good actor can make the audience believe a block of wood is a sword, a Coarse Actor can make them believe a sword is a block of wood.

A useful variation is shown in the pictures. This has the advantage of being even safer. In this the combatants do not use their swords at all, but circle round and then rush together, lock sword hilts and rest their shields against each other's shield. They grunt copiously, break, and repeat the whole movement as required.

The fatal thrust is important. I suppose there is no way of improving upon the normal method of thrusting the sword under the opponent's armpit, but this scares me so much that I spend the fight with one arm held out horizontally (see picture).

It is perfectly satisfactory to dispense with the fatal thrust altogether. Why should it matter if one man collapses for no reason? Better still, let both swordsmen contrive to work their way off stage, where after a loud yell the winner can return with red toothpaste all over his hands.

These methods have been tried and tested over the years on thousands of stages ranging from Stratford-on-Avon and the National Theatre to the smallest rep, not forgetting BBC TV. So have nothing to do with a director who wishes to abandon tradition and introduce realism. Besides, realism can be dangerous to people such as Askew, who is so scared he spends every fight cringing behind his shield.

As you value your life, never allow a fencing expert near rehearsals.

I shall never forget a schools production of *Henry IV*, Part One, in which the school fencing champion played a part. The audience cowered in their seats as his sword whirled flashing arcs over the edge of the stage. Not only the audience, but most of the actors cowered too. That valiant Cock o' the North Hotspur didn't even put up a fight. He just shrank into a corner and waited to be killed.

And it is of little practical value to engage a fencing expert. After hours wasted practising mid-air ripostes and suchlike it will all revert to normal on the night, and people will be slain by thrusts in the most unlikely places.

Apart from anything else there is always the danger that a realistic fight will become too heated, especially if there is a little bad blood between the actors involved. Askew was once miscast as Vasques in *'Tis Pity She's a Whore*. Unfortunately Grimaldi, whom Vasques has to kill, was not only a violent man but he loathed Askew. The result was that when poor Askew went to slay him rather tentatively the man attacked him with such violence that Askew fled from the stage, bleeding at the forehead.

The difficulty now was to have Grimaldi killed. Finally the stage manager succeeded in hissing from the wings 'Die', and he took the hint and died. But even then Askew circled warily round his body.

The same technique should be applied to fist fights as to sword fights. Never mind the director, just go into a harmless clinch and grunt. Don't believe any maniac who says that no blow hurts if you ride it. I have seen this theory tried out in rehearsal and it took half an hour to bring the man round.

If you have the misfortune to play a part which requires you to be struck on the head with a club insist on personally inspecting the weapon before the performance. Some property mistresses will provide a club like a young railway sleeper. It is, of course, possible to make a hollow club with a tongue of wood on a spring inside which will give out a realistic sound at the slightest tap. If props have provided one like this I have only this piece of advice:

Throw it away, preferably in the direction of the person who made it.

Alternatively, try it out on the head of the director. These things invariably go wrong and deliver a stunning blow. In fact the safest thing is to make your own club out of string, cloth and old newspaper. It won't sound very realistic, but you'll survive.

As a matter of general advice, if ever doubtful about a piece of dangerous business always try it on the director. Pretend not to understand what he requires and ask him to demonstrate.

'I'm sorry, Ron, I don't quite understand how I ride the blow when he pushes the broken bottle in my face . . . I wonder if you'd just show me'.

It's surprising how quickly these things are dropped when that technique is adopted.

If a fight ends in death be sure to die in a comfortable position. Once again ignore any director who wants an actor to hang around for half a scene draped over a grandfather clock or some such nonsense. My advice to the aspiring body is to die behind something and then have a good sleep. If one is in view there is always the danger of heavy breathing or even a sneeze, apart from the strain of having to lie still (see pictures, ways of dying).

Coarse death, like Coarse sword-fighting, is traditional. No matter where the wound is, the pain is always felt in the bowels. I have lost count of the sword fights I've seen where the thrust is under the armpit and the victim clutches his navel and doubles up. The symptoms of poisoning, stabbing, shooting and bludgeoning are all similar – the actor should seize the bowels firmly and sink down with a gurgle. This gives great opportunities for Coarse Actors, some of whom become expert at making their final gurgles last for a long time. No one can interfere, because it looks odd if another character interrupts a death throe. A useful wheeze is to appear to die and then start up again just as someone else speaks.

Have nothing to do with sadistic directors who want a death with blood all over the stage, directors who expect an actor to go through a scene with a bladder of fake blood hidden in his bosom or lie by the footlights with a sword sticking vertically out of his stomach. The sword will undoubtedly start to teeter slowly to the ground, mesmerizing the audience, while the fake-blood idea may well result in the Unpleasantnesses which occurred to Askew's cousin Watkins, whose blood-container developed a leak long before he was due to die, so he appeared to have a haemorrhage in the middle of his dinner.

Finally a little advice on the curtain call.

My first words are simply never take one. To start with, the curtain in an amateur theatre is an embarrassment, being the worst-organized part of the show, rehearsed for the first time at about eleven o'clock the previous night. At the best the curtain will either stick or rise for a hastily milked third call to reveal everyone tiptoeing off or making rude signs at the audience.

At the worst there will be one of these clever types of call in which everyone tramps round in a procession that goes on and on until the audience are exhausted with clapping, so those coming on last enter to silence.

Apart from anything else, a curtain call may make you late for the boozer.

It is a poor Coarse Actor who cannot be in the pub by the time the curtain comes down, unless he is due on stage at the end of the play.

However, if you have the misfortune to have to take a curtain at least use the opportunity to draw attention to yourself. One method, especially suitable for women, is to pass a hand across the brow, totter feebly, regain composure with an obvious effort, and collapse as the curtain comes to. This has the added advantage of cutting the ground from under the feet of critics. Obviously you were under strain the whole evening.

More unusual, but quite effective, is to break ranks, march to the leading man and shake him warmly by the hand (or kiss the leading lady). No one will know why you have done this but the audience will think you must be important.*

* This may seem incredible, but I once played with a man who was in such a hurry to get home he used to put on bicycle clips for the curtain call. He could never understand why the audience laughed.

5

Be Prepared

'And in the next-door room is heard the tramp
And "rhubarb, rhubarb" as the crowd rehearse. . . .'
JOHN BETJEMAN (Summoned by Bells)

Trapped on stage – the pistol which wouldn't – how not to give a prompt – the Unpleasantness at Northampton – collapse of elderly theatre

The most important thing a Coarse Actor can master is a knowledge of some common crises which are liable to arise on stage. By anticipating a crisis he can often come out of the situation with an advantage over more talented players. There is no question as to whether a crisis will arise. Law Three of Coarse Acting states: 'Every production will be accompanied by a crisis.' It is a sign of inexperience to believe a show can go on without a hitch.

How often does one hear an actor say in rehearsal something like: 'I know one night you're going to drop that blasted vase.' Yet how many actors trouble to prepare for the inevitable dropping? Directors would be much better advised to spend the time rehearsing what to do when something goes wrong than in keeping the cast standing around discussing obscure points of interpretation, such as whether the chief character is in love with his aunt (or even his uncle).

DOORS AND EXITS. Doors are troublesome objects (Law 4: 'Scenery doors are not designed to close or to open'). There is little that can be done about the door which slowly swings open during a scene unless one gets up and shuts it, in which case it will almost certainly swing open again. Good for a laugh, but not much else. I do not advise the stage manager to reach his hand round and pull it shut unless he is at loggerheads with the director and wishes to gain revenge by spoiling the show.

Worse, however, is the door that won't open, so an actor can't get on, and, even worse, the door that won't let anyone off, so you wander desperately around looking for a way of escape. In the first part I ever played (as a schoolboy in *Goodbye Mr Chips* at the old Leicester Theatre Royal) I even tried to go out of a door that was painted on a flat. I must have looked stupid clawing at the canvas with my nails; Mr Chips, who was supposed to be dying, had to get up and show me the way out.

Never force a door. Have you ever seen an entire box set slowly teeter inwards and bury Professor Higgins? If you have (as I have) then you will not viciously tug at a door that refuses to budge.

If a door will not open the best thing to do is to look for another exit. It is usually possible to squeeze out between the proscenium arch and the tormentor, or even through the orchestra pit.

*Do not escape through the fireplace as this is unrealistic.**

Should no other exit be available the stranded actor must let the rest of the cast know of his predicament. Have a line ready in keeping with the play. For a comedy one might say, 'The jolly old door has jammed', but in a thriller it would be more appropriate to bellow, 'My God, the swine have nailed up our only way of escape!'

An alert stage manager will realize from this that something has gone wrong and will at once start levering at the door from back stage.

With an efficient stage manager these simple precautions should be enough, although I recollect one SM who simply picked up the offending door off its hinges and walked away with it. A desperate expedient, but effective.

PISTOLS, ETC. Stage pistols and firearms do not work.

This is not stated as opinion but fact. A special type of pistol is issued to amateurs. I never knew an amateur performance in which the shot came in the right place, if it came

* Unless playing Father Christmas

at all. Presume as a matter of course that if a pistol has to be fired on stage it will not go off, or if one is being fired in the wings that will not go off either.

My friend Askew, after uselessly clicking his pistol half a dozen times, suddenly leaped on his astonished victim and finished him off with a knife from the sideboard. As he did so there was a loud bang from the wings where the stage manager had got the emergency gun to work. This was rather different from the Unpleasantness at Leeds, where the victim, realizing the pistol had misfired, saved the situation by falling down with a cry of, 'Poisoned, by God!'

It is a good idea for the killer and the victim to get together and decide who is to say the emergency words. What must be avoided is for *both* of them to say the emergency lines, so the victim totters around crying, 'The whisky had cyanide in it, you swine', while the murderer is shouting, 'Another victim for my new, silent Mauser automatic!'

A further wheeze is for the victim to let out a great shout as the killer raises his gun. If he shouts loudly enough, it may conceal the pitiful absence of any explosion.

The jinx on stage firearms is really quite astonishing. It hardly seems possible than an entire firing squad should all misfire, yet I saw it occur at a Left Wing theatre producing a play about the Spanish Civil War. The hero had made the conventional farewell speech (one of the conventions being that during this oration all the soldiers face outwards and threaten the audience with their rifles) and then the firing squad lined up. As the hero shouted his final defiance there came a series of little clicks and the hero was left calling defiance on the Fascists until the curtain mercifully came down.

CRÊPE HAIR. A good stage manager will always have a lick of spirit gum handy in the wings, and keep one eye open for the danger signs of a flagging moustache or a weary beard. A treasure of a stage manager once saved me from utter disgrace by perceiving that my ample moustache was coming off, and beckoning to me from the wings to work my way off stage for an emergency repair. In addition she crept round behind the scenery whispering my lines to me. I always regretted that she married someone else, because I am sure we could have made a go of it if that was an example of her beautiful nature and resourceful mind.

COLLAPSE OF SCENERY. A Coarse production rarely passes without the collapse of part of the set, be it merely a small portion of the fireplace or an entire wall.

If this happens do not panic.

A quick-witted Coarse Actor, upon seeing a teetering flat, will immediately walk across and lean up against it, even if this means missing his exit, until the offending scenery is secured from back stage.

One of the finest speeches I have ever heard was made by an Othello holding up a pillar which threatened to crush the recumbent Desdemona. He had to do his strangling at long range from by the pillar, and very well he did it too.

Should it not be possible to prop up the scenery in time, one can at least have a suitable line ready for after the collapse. I personally find it effective simply to say 'Woodworm' rather laconically when the dust has settled.

It is, however, a law of Coarse Theatre that scenery which is *meant* to collapse will never do so. It is all very well for R. C. Sheriff to write in the stage directions for *Journey's End*:

The shelling has risen to a great fury. The solitary candle burns with a steady flame, and Raleigh lies in the shadows. The whine of a shell rises to a shriek and bursts on the dugout roof. The shock stabs out the candle-flame; the timber-props of the door cave slowly in, sandbags fall and block the passage to the open air . . .

But that is exactly what will not happen on the night.

In a Coarse production the wretched dugout will collapse in the first scene without a shot being fired, and will then obstinately refuse to show even the smallest sign of weakness at the end, when it ought to cave in.

One of the saddest things I have ever experienced in a play was to see Watkins screaming in the middle of the stage: 'Mercy . . . mercy . . . the whole house is falling about my ears. . . .'

At this point the ceiling was supposed to collapse. He was still repeating the line five minutes later while teams of stage-hands sweated with jammed ropes and pulleys.

Eventually they brought the curtain down, and the vile ceiling promptly fell on the heads of the cast while they were taking the curtain call.

UNEXPECTED APPEARANCE OF STRANGE CHARACTERS. Be prepared for people to appear on stage who are not supposed to be in that scene. They may wander about trying to say lines and can become abusive until they realize their error, which should be pointed out by another actor in a whisper. Do not try to attract their attention from the wings or they will stare fixedly off-stage scratching their heads, or else give a hoarse cry of alarm.

Even more alarming is for people to appear on the stage who are not in the show, a hazard to which performances in public halls are particularly vulnerable. A policeman once marched on-stage in a London suburb and demanded to know who owned a car which was blocking the entrance. The play stopped immediately, since the owner was one of the actresses. Another time I was at a village hall when a doctor wandered through the scenery into the middle of a murder mystery. Someone in the audience had fainted and they'd phoned for him and he'd come in the back way. On this occasion, though, the cast tried to continue, but the doctor became irritated at being ignored and asked to see the patient in a commanding voice.

It was then the actor playing the detective committed one of the bravest deeds I have seen in the theatre. Realizing the doctor must be got rid of at all costs he stepped forward and boomed, 'I think you have a lot of explaining to do, Doctor – or should I call you Major Fairfax?' With which, he dragged the wretched medic into the wings and handed him over to the stage manager.

CHARACTER FAILING TO APPEAR. Don't waste time gagging. Go off stage and fetch him. He will probably be found gossiping in the wings or playing cards in the dressing-room.

Warning: An actor in Birmingham was watching from the wings when there was a hiatus on stage. Realizing someone had failed to make an appearance he ran to the dressing-room to fetch him, when he discovered the missing person was himself.

INTERFERENCE FROM AUDIENCE. The smallness of amateur theatres and halls makes Coarse Acting especially prone to this hazard. The interference can range from the evil schoolboy who grabs the bottom of a cloak to the old dear who puts her tea-cup on stage. Not to mention the child who recognizes his parent and bleats loudly, 'Why is that man sticking that sword into my daddy?'

Included among the hazards must be the case of the talkative front row who are not above addressing the actors directly. It is most disconcerting to come on stage and hear a voice say loudly, 'Here comes that man you don't like, Mum.'

Just as bad was the lady who once leant forward from the front row and said, 'You've dropped your glasses.' I knew I had dropped them, it was a subtle part of the plot which nobody was supposed to notice, and here was this idiot booming it all over the auditorium.

Amateur audiences also feel that they have a *carte blanche* to express their disapproval publicly. In one Pinter play every night we used to play a game of guessing who had walked out.

'That's the Chief Constable,' Askew would whisper to me as there was the sound of a seat being violently tipped up and a disturbance in the audience. Someone else would say no, it was Councillor Frogworthy, he always walked out when sex was discussed.

The strangest interruption from the audience that I can recall came because of a prop. Someone had lent us a violin. It looked merely a broken-down old fiddle and we treated it rather roughly. On the third night of the run, during a scene where two people wrestled for possession of the instrument, one of the actors had the brilliant idea of hitting the other on the head with the violin. It broke.

Immediately a wail arose from somewhere out front and a formidable woman stood up.

'How dare you treat my violin like that,' she boomed. 'Do you understand that it is over fifty years old?'

Well, we tried to carry on as if nothing was happening, while everyone cried 'Sssh', but the woman would not stop.

'Look at you,' she shouted, 'you've not even said you're sorry. And now you've put it on that chair where someone will sit on it.' (That was the whole idea.)

At the interval she marched back stage and demanded the return of the violin. This was unfortuante because it had a key part in the next act, but she insisted and we went through the rest of play with a violin hastily constructed from a piece of broom handle and some cardboard.

CLOUD OF STEAM ENTERING AUDITORIUM. An unusual crisis, but experienced at more than one hall. It is caused when the refreshment tea is being made near to a door into the auditorium. Two minutes from the interval the door will open, a cloud of steam will obscure the audience and a female voice will boom: 'Is it the interval yet?'

The odd thing is that however much the timing of a show changes, the steam-laden apparition will appear at the same spot each night, almost as if she had a cue for it. As it is impossible to compete with a cloud of vapour, there is nothing that can be done except to keep calm.

Do not answer the question about the interval.

My worst experience of refreshment staff was in *The Mikado*. Towards the interval the tempo got slower and slower, until Poo Bah hissed at the conductor, 'What's the matter?'

Back came the reply, 'They want to hold back the interval. The water's not boiled yet.'

CURTAIN FALLING IN MIDDLE OF SCENE. This is quite likely to occur if there is a line in the scene similar to the curtain line. In fact it is quite liable to happen even if there is no such line. It is best not to take up the curtain immediately, as this would indicate that the whole thing was a mistake. Instead, wait for about half a minute, and the audience may think it was a genuine break. An actor on stage when this happens should control himself and not indicate surprise or dismay when the curtain starts to come to. Under no circumstances try to hold it back physically.

The converse of this disaster is for the curtain to rise unexpectedly, or more frequently for a black-out to end too soon. It is best simply to assume that all black-outs will end before the cast are settled and then one is prepared for the worst. Once again the curse of acting in the round is well illustrated by the unfortunate experience of Askew's sister Maureen, who failed to get off stage in an exit black-out and suddenly found herself alone in the acting area when the lights went up, with people selling tea all about her.

INTERVAL COMING IN WRONG PLACE. An unusual hazard, but one I have experienced at a fringe theatre. It was an experimental work by an unknown author, and consisted largely of black-outs and grunts. The house manager mistook one of the black-outs for the interval and immediately switched on the house lights and started marching up and down the aisles selling ice-cream. Meanwhile the actors were in full swing again. The poor author stood up in the auditorium and bellowed that it was all a mistake, how could the swine eat ice-cream while his play was going on, etc. etc., but nobody paid any attention.

FORGETTING LINES. This is the commonest Coarse Acting crisis of all, so it deserves close attention.

It is important to remember that it is no use to rely on the prompter, even if there is one, which is by no means certain. However, if there is a prompter the first duty of any Coarse Actor is to ascertain his/her position, so that in case of emergency one can work to the prompt side and whisper, 'Yes m'dear', out of the corner of the mouth.

In this respect it is essential to keep in character. For instance, in an Elizabethan play one could mutter, 'Yea coz?' so the audience might think it part of the play.

Remember that a clumsy march across the stage is worse than useless. The essence of the operation is to move firmly yet subtly. If possible try to find some business for taking you right across the stage.

After all this it may be rather disconcerting to find that the prompt has moved to the other side of the stage. Try to urge on her that she *must* stay in the same place. These girls have a habit of wandering, especially if they have a crush on the lighting man or some other back-stage official.

Of course, whatever one does is no use if the prompt is half-witted. On one of the many occasions on which I have dried, the voice of the prompter, a keen young girl with spectacles, rang out loud and clear. It was such a change to have an audible prompt that I nearly applauded, only what she said was not much use. She simple said:

'And.'

Well, that wasn't enough, so I sidled off towards her and when near enough hissed, 'And what?'

'And the . . .' came the reply.

In the end I had to go off stage and seize the book from her.

But her colleague was even worse. Every time anyone fluffed she sat watching the book and saying nothing, merely nodding to herself wisely. When the actor finally made an attempt at the line she looked up, wagged her finger and said, 'Wrong . . . wrong . . . nearly right. . . .'

If you are sufficiently *en rapport* with another member of the cast you might have an agreement that he learns your lines as well as his own, while you do the same favour for him, This is not such a strange suggestion as it sounds, because one of the symptoms of a Coarse Actor is that he always knows other people's lines and never his own.

Kenneth More tells in his book *Kindly Leave the Stage* how he saved a colleague from disaster by knowing both sets of lines. The poor fellow was playing a jailer, come to tell More details of his execution. Alas, he opened the cell door and dried completely, so More got the dialogue from him by question and answer:

'I expect you have come to tell me the details of my execution?'

'Er . . . yes . . .'

'It will be a horrible death, will it not?'

'Er . . . yes . . .'

'And afterwards I shall be hung up for the birds to eat?'

'Probably . . .'

'And buried in unconsecrated ground?'

'Definitely . . .'

But this is a technique only for the experienced.

In opera and musical shows, drying is less of a problem because the audience frequently can't hear the words anyway.

If stuck, one can usually get away with a sort of meaningless groaning, an all-purpose Coarse lyric noise which comes out like, 'Hooly hong, I hah hee, ace eeh harch. . . .' When the chorus come in, try to pick up the gist of the song from them. As a last resort simply sing; 'I love you', repeatedly. It fits most duets.

I have already referred to the kindly stage manager who followed me round the stage whispering my lines from behind the scenery, and I would recommend this method as the only certain one. Of course, not all stage managers are as tractable, but it should be possible to bribe some kind-hearted props girl with little to do to follow you around stage from the back.*

Askew is one of the few people I know who has actually taken a prompt from the audience. Apparently there was someone in the front row who knew the play (or at least knew it better than he did, which would not have been difficult) and he was astounded to hear his line floating up from the auditorium. His astonishment, however, did not prevent him from accepting the prompt with gratitude. He has been looking for the person ever since with the intention of paying him a small fee to attend every performance. Beware of the evil-minded actor who forgets his own lines and throws the blame on the person opposite, usually by asking some question that isn't in the script.

An old pro I knew used to have a stock speech ready for this emergency. If it was a Shakespeare play, he would stare the offender in the eye and say firmly:

> 'Thou weariest me.
> Unto my chamber shall I now retire
> And rest me on my couch a little hour.
> Farewell, until we meet again, farewell.'

He would then exit, light a cigarette in the wings and watch his victim trying to get out of that one.

Some producers work on the theory that if there is no prompt then nobody will dry.

NEVER TAKE PART IN ANY SUCH PRODUCTION.

I hang my head in shame at the Unpleasantness in

* In amateur musicals, the conductor has been known to give the line.

All-purpose Coarse
expression: love, joy,
pleasure, hope etc.

All-purpose Coarse
expression (female):
hate, grief etc. Can
also be used to
indicate physical
illness, indigestion
etc.

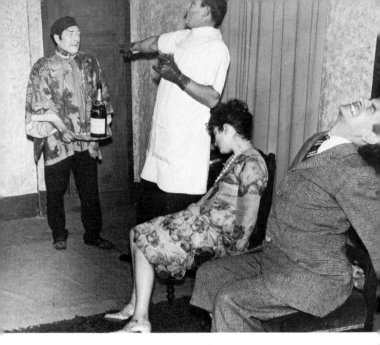

Above: How to steal a scene, though unconscious.

Right: Simple sword fight. The Eternal Parry. This can be carried on for as long as required.

Above: Normal method of killing.

Left: A pleasant and harmless alternative way of conducting a sword fight. Both contestants should stay locked in this position, grunting occasionally. To terminate the fight, one of the characters should drop dead.

Left: Wrong way to die. This pose is impossible to hold. Also the knife will slowly teeter to the floor.

Below left: Right way to die. All is ease and comfort.

Above right: Right way to take a prompt. An historic photograph taken during an actual performance of my friend Askew at the moment of forgetting his lines. Why are his eyes closed? Because he is trying to listen to the lighting man hissing the line. The real prompt came ten seconds later.

Right: Wrong way to take a prompt.

Basic all-purpose
Coarse costume
(female), suitable for
any period and any
part with fewer than
six lines.

Basic all-purpose
Coarse costume
(female) with
sixteenth/seventeenth/
eighteenth-century
additions.

The author wearing all-purpose Coarse costume.

If photographs of your society's productions look like this, then you may consider yourself Coarse Actors.

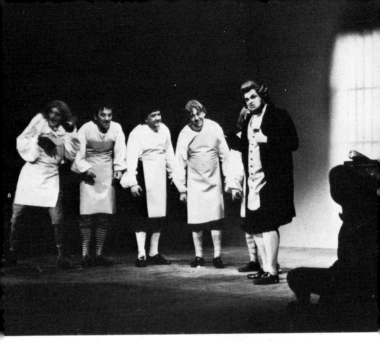

The man on the left
has read this book.

This is Askew's cousin,
Watkins, playing
some part or other,
but I don't know
which. Probably Lord
Scroop or someone
similar. Note the
subtlety of the make-up.
This actor could
never go unnoticed.

Northampton when we were playing *The Servant of Two Masters* in the open-air without a prompt. Not only did we do it without a prompt but without half of the second act one night, thanks to a combination of myself and the man playing opposite. We are still trying to decide who was to blame.

PLAY GOING ROUND IN CIRCLES. Another common danger. It occurs when a character has similar lines at different parts in the play and saying the second line triggers off an automatic response in another actor who says the reply from the earlier part and the whole thing starts again. Watkins swears he saw a production in which someone tore off their false beard and immediately there came a line similar to one earlier, they all went back ten minutes, and the man had to replace his beard.

AMNESIA. Forgetting who you are is not uncommon. At least twice I have entered and said something like, 'My liege, I am—', or 'Good morning, my name is—' and suddenly realized I've forgotten who the hell I'm supposed to be. So always write the character's name on your wrist. This will also avoid the unpleasantness which occurs when you're playing several parts and you introduce yourself by the wrong name.

COLLAPSE OF THEATRE. Not a frequent occurrence except in areas subject to earthquakes, although I can remember a great chunk of plaster bursting like a bomb in the audience. The sight, however, of half the audience evacuating their seats owing to a leak in the roof is by no means unknown. Above all, keep calm and do not hold out a hand to see if it is raining. Askew claims that a theatre really did collapse about him a few years ago. He was playing in a large marquee which fell down in the third act, burying actors and audience alike.

MEGALOMANIA OF SHAKESPEAREAN KINGS. I have been a servant to seven English monarchs, cup-bearer to the King of Denmark, messenger to the rulers of France and Bohemia, bodyguard to the Queen of Egypt and close attendant upon the Doge of Venice. All upon the stage, of course. I've been stabbed by kings (once when it wasn't in the script), hanged by kings, tortured by kings, rewarded by kings and in *Richard III* something quite unmentionable happened to me. But it's what happens off-stage that I wish to warn about. Believe me, wearing the cardboard crown has no small effect on these monarchs of the outer suburbs, which is quite understandable when you consider that for rehearsal period of maybe six weeks they spend nearly every evening condemning people to death and kicking grovelling messengers around (or in the case of queens, being wooed by six monarchs at once).

The king's attitude begins to harden during rehearsals. There is a tendency to ask courtiers and clowns to fetch props or run errands. But the megalomania bursts forth completely at dress rehearsal when he stands twitching neurotically in the dressing-room, surrounded by attendants changing the royal armour, doing up the royal surcoat, carrying rude messages to the stage manager and returning with even ruder ones. On the first night the king can bear no one near him, except for an occasional slave to fetch aspirins and brandy. To disobey is unthinkable – the habits of six weeks' rehearsal are too strong.

Worry not. The king's reign is short. On the last night rebellion will rear its head, and the kings sense it. They start trying to be friendly and offer to buy drinks. Now, if the king has over-played his hand he is liable to be subjected to pranks. The cider in the royal cup may be replaced with ink, or part of the crown removed. The game is up. Tonight dies royal Richard, tomorrow he becomes Mr Smith of Sidcup who is rather interested in amateur dramatics. Watching a stage king return to reality always reminds me of that quotation about Charles I, '. . . saddest of all kings, crowned and again discrowned. . . .' There is something to be said for being a Coarse Actor after all. The return to reality is so much less shattering.

6 The Director

'The notes taken by the director as he silently watches the players are a test of his competence. If, for example, he writes: "The Oedipus Complex must be very apparent here. Discuss with the Queen", the sooner he is packed out of the theatre and replaced, the better.'
BERNARD SHAW

Those who can't, direct – Unpleasantness in London – a howl in the night – don't bother about the author – when to be horrid to the cast – the Diary of a Disaster

The first quality that a director, or producer as they used to be known, must have is an inability to act. Given that blockage to the expression of his/her personality, it naturally follows that if a person is still keen to impose something on the stage then they had better direct.

Lack of talent is no bar to becoming a successful director with an amateur society. Modesty is the greatest handicap. It is not necessary to know anything about drama or the theatre, but it is absolutely essential to give the impression of knowing everything.

The sort of talk which never impresses an amateur group is the good old plain man-o'-the-boards stuff ('Quite honestly, I reckon a director's first duty is to get 'em out of each other's way and make 'em speak up.'). Anything practical and down-to-earth like that dooms a director from the start. The society pseuds will soon be saying, 'He must have been in rep at one time', which is not a compliment in the world of the pseud.

It is preferred, even in the lower strata of the amateur dramatic world, if one talks in vague phrases that mean nothing. For example, one might say: 'Believe me, I am not interested in the mere mechanics of speech. It is immaterial whether the audience hear my actors speaking, but it is absolutely essential that they should hear them *thinking*.'

Having been chosen, however, a Coarse director must set about casting his play. It is essential to have a reading for parts. This, of course, will be completely disregarded as a basis of casting a play, which has already been done over pints of bitter and cups of coffee elsewhere, but justice must appear to be done. If anyone should complain, the director can always say, 'I didn't like your reading, ducky.'

But a word of warning. Shun the casting couch.

Any director who would cast a woman merely because he has hopes of her favours is simply a human rat, devoid of morals. Not only that, but you stand a much better chance of success with women if you don't cast them. Once their object is achieved by being cast, their attitude changes rapidly and they will produce an incredibly good-looking young man at rehearsals, with whom it appears they have been madly in love for years.

Although the casting couch should be eschewed, there is no need to forego the casting pint. I kept myself in free drinks one winter by dropping hints to people that they looked just right for the lead in my next show. Actually, I wasn't directing anything at all, but they still kept buying me drink.

In reality, of course, few directors have a really free hand in casting. In many societies certain parts are in the gift of certain people, rather like rectorships in rural parishes. Even tiny servant roles are sometimes the prerogative of wizened little men who help with the lighting when Fred's ill. As to whether these local traditions are followed depends on whether you wish to direct there again. Sometimes it is rather fun to stir things up a little and depart, leaving them all at each other's throats.

However, there is one exception to this, and that is the show, usually produced by a works or office dramatic society, for which the director is paid. In that case there is only one choice for a man of honour, and that is to cast the play exactly as the committee would like it cast. After all, they *are* paying you, and they're doing the show for their own amusement, not for yours, and certainly not for the audience's.

A director may well be ignored in any case. Askew often tells how he was directing a show for a firm in London and he cast a clerk in the lead and the chief accountant as a walk-on.

At the first rehearsal he was surprised to see the chief accountant reading the clerk's lines. When asked what was going on, the accountant replied meaningly, 'We've decided to change parts. You don't mind, do you?'

Since the whole production is merely an extension of the welfare department I can never take one of these shows seriously. Money is rarely any object, scenery and costumes are hired wholesale and the whole affair is graced by the drunken presence of a few senior executives on the first night.

These distinguish themselves by arriving halfway through the first act and leaving for the bar at the first interval, returning noisily just before the curtain falls. When this happens the senior executive will lurch on stage, breathing gin fumes over everyone and make a speech saying how wonderful it all was.

The only time I have ever enjoyed a firm's play was when I directed one for a West End store, and while the managing director was making his speech ('And we mustn't forget those boys and girls who worked so hard back stage') one of the boys and girls who worked so hard back stage let the curtain fall on his head and felled him to the ground.

The chap who did it told me afterwards that they later transferred him to the hardware department, which was apparently considered the final indignity.

IMPORTANT WARNING: Never cast your wife in your own show unless you desire everyone to say, 'Oh yes, we all know how she got the part.'

However, let us assume the casting of the play is complete. The director must now consider his approach to the whole thing. If he is wise he will adopt one rule in dealing with a Coarse cast – be as simple as possible.

With sorrow and sadistic pleasure I recall the fine directors I have seen reduced to gibbering madness by the built-in obstinacy of amateur companies and back-stage staffs. I remember years ago trying to cope with a women's institute.

I wanted a woman who was supposed to have just received a shattering shock to give a ghastly, inhuman wail off stage. I wanted the cry of a soul in anguish, the half-human sob of a woman at the end of her tether.

I don't think we rehearsed anything for six weeks except

that blasted sob. The first time she did it, it sounded as if someone was being sick in the wings. At other rehearsals she simply stood there and bellowed like a cow in pain. In the end I said we had better cut the sob, and she went all sullen and said she was just getting it, and it was helping her feel the part.

On the first night I carefully left the Memorial Hall before the sob came, and went for a drink. I was just about to enter the bar when from the hall came an indescribable shriek which froze my hand on the door and echoed through the silent village night. The shriek was followed by a chorus of barks and bellows from every farm for miles around.

The landlord asked me anxiously if I'd heard that ghastly sound outside and I confessed I'd not only heard, I was partly responsible for it. He thought I was joking.

Once I read John Bourne's excellent book *Teach Yourself Amateur Acting*. I read it on the advice of a director who drew me gently aside and said: 'Michael, I want to recommend you a book on acting. Please promise me you'll read it, dear boy. It might help you to stop waving your arms about.'

Mr Bourne quotes as an example of inventive business the scene in *They Came to a City* where Joe sits and talks and smokes. Mr Bourne suggests that he should roll his own cigarette instead of merely lighting one.

Now this is just the sort of extra business a Coarse director must avoid. It's bad enough when a Coarse Actor has merely to light a cigarette – the trembling hand, the match which won't strike, the frantic puffing at a dead cigarette – but to roll one would be a disaster. He would probably finish up with tobacco all over the stage and a snake-like object in his mouth which would go up in flames the minute he lit it.

The most a Coarse director can hope for from his cast is that they will get on stage somewhere around the cue, say their lines more or less accurately, or, if not their own lines, someone else's, and then exit without knocking over the scenery. Instructions should therefore be kept as simple as possible. It is no use asking for the sound of a man in spiritual torment. At least, you can ask for it, but you won't get it. What you will receive might be recorded for use as a fog signal, but that's about all.

Directions to the cast should be reduced to the following:

SPEAK LOUDER	SPEAK SOFTER
SPEAK SLOWER	SPEAK QUICKER
MOVE LEFT	MOVE RIGHT
MOVE DOWN STAGE	MOVE UP STAGE

And the average Coarse Actor has difficulty even in grasping those. If no directions at all are given it can generally be assumed that he will mumble unintelligibly and mask someone.

A director will usually find that all his energies are taken up with the sheer mechanics of keeping some sort of order among the cast and getting through the rehearsals. It will help him to do this if he remembers the techniques which it is possible to use.

A. The Ingratiating Technique: 'Now that was wonderful, boys and girls, absolutely wonderful. Sheila dear, I must say I was a teeny-weeny bit surprised when you sat down for your big speech. . . . Yes, dear, I know you were tired, but you see it's more effective standing up. . . . No, no, no, I'm not criticizing you, darling, honestly I thought the delivery was just terrific. Possibly a deaf person sitting at the back of the hall might not have heard every single syllable, hmmmm? . . .'

B. Hail-fellow-well-met Technique: 'Right, gather round, everybody. Bert, hand me a fag and that bottle of beer, will you? Now listen, darlings, that was all right. Fine. OK. We've got a production here, we've definitely got a show, boys and girls. Honestly I laughed my head off. Fred, that bit of business when you fell flat on your face was just fine . . . fine. But don't overdo it, mate. Cut that idea of getting your head stuck in the wedding cake. You old ham [*punching him*], you're just an old scene-stealer. No, I love it. . . .'

C. The professional (who's doing it as a favour since he lives nearby): It is not possible to quote from him because he says little in rehearsals apart from an occasional snarl. He never addresses the cast as a whole except to announce an extra rehearsal on Saturday afternoon, and then throw a fit when someone says he can't come because he's playing cricket.

Sometimes he will treat actors and actresses to a stream of vituperation, provided he knows they won't answer back. On the first night he gets drunk and tells everyone how good they are and how he is asking his friends from the BBC down to see the show. They never come.

In an effort to impress, a director is perfectly entitled to mangle an author's script as much as he likes. Anyone in the publishing business will confirm that authors are lower than dirt, anyway. Just for guidance, the order of seniority in a play goes as follows:

> Man who puts up the money (professionals only)
> Lighting or wardrobe departments
> Set designers and constructors
> Stage management
> Treasurer of the society
> Leading actors
> The director
> Coarse actors
> Theatre cat
> The author

The very pinnacles of the Stage have set the example of wrecking an author's work, from the time when Colley Cibber started pepping up Shakespeare (among other things he added the line 'Off with his head' in *Richard III*). Of course, if he had been a modern director he would have changed the locale to Italy as well.

Only recently I played in one of those what's-the-use-it's-all-hopeless types of plays, written by an aspiring local author, which ended in utter misery, like this:

ALF: It's all a rotten, stinking cheat. That's all life is. A dirty word. It takes your youth and your hopes and your dreams, shatters them and leaves you a prisoner in a sick, ageing body to drag out the remains of a weary existence until you die horribly in a seedy lodging-house. Oh God, how I hate myself.

Enter Gert, his girl friend

GERT: Alf?

ALF: Get out, you stupid bitch.

He sobs uncontrollably, She screams and rushes off. There is a sound of a shot off stage. Alf lifts his head, pulls a bottle of sleeping tablets from his pocket and starts to stuff them into his mouth as

> *The curtain falls*

The director rewrote this to read:

ALF: Sometimes I wonder what life is all about. If only there was some hope somewhere.

> *Enter Gert*

GERT: Alf?

ALF: Gert . . . you've come back . . . I knew you would, darling. Together we can fact the future . . .

> *They stand looking at each other tenderly as the curtain falls*

As I was only playing a bus-conductor I didn't mind, but the poor author was almost deranged. Nobody had the courtesy to tell him of the alterations, so the first he knew about them was at the opening night, when he interrupted the curtain by coming on stage and taking a swing at the leading man. Then he persuaded his agents to send us a stream of rude letters and writs and injunctions. Not that it did any good. The well-established rule of TV, radio and the stage is that the last person to know anything about a work of art is the person who writes it.

Occasionally lines really do need altering, but for some reason directors will never amend the lines which genuinely need attention. Askew and I used to go into fits every night at the rehearsals of a play which contained the lines:

'Has the Doctor seen her, Fanny?'

'Yes, and he said there was little hope.'

The actress who said the first line invariably omitted the comma, but the director saw nothing wrong. He simply put on a twisted smile and said he didn't think everyone had peculiar minds like ours. The result was that on the first night the show stopped at that point with the audience in tears of mirth and crying out for mercy.

A further act of rewriting that may be needed is to amend the play to accommodate fifty extra people. This especially applies in musicals. In societies with more acting members than there are parts to go round, it is often customary to squeeze in the surplus at all costs, even if it means amending whole chunks of the play. A long-standing friend tells how when he was in *The Desert Song* at Leeds he was astonished when thirty or forty extra Arabs—mostly women—wandered on stage for the second verse of one of his numbers. 'They were literally coming out of the rocks', he told me. The extras then sang the rest of the song with him (despite the fact it was supposed to be a solo) and disappeared into the rocks again.

The most horrible example of this, however, was a production of *My Fair Lady* in which a complete dream sequence was written in. While Eliza sat in Professor Higgins's room all her old Cockney friends passed by the window, one by one, singing and leering at her. As this society had an enormous acting membership the procession took about half an hour. I'm sure some went round twice.

Having mutilated the play to your satisfaction, it may now be blocked. As an author's lines are fair game, so are his situations. After all, one must ensure that the audience know some sort of direction has gone into the thing.

The classics, in particular, are easy meat for a nice spot of mutilation and as these days it does not seem to matter how the verse is spoken there is endless opportunity for showing how superior the director is to the unfortunate author.

Part of a typical mangled production of *Macbeth* might well go something like this:

> *Enter Macbeth. He prowls round the stage eating an apple.*

MACBETH: If—

> *He throws the apple core out of the window.*

Itwurdunwentisduntwere
WELL·
(*A raven is heard croaking.*)
Twere done.
(*He turns an hour-glass upside down.*)
Quickly if the assassination could
(*A dog walks across the stage. He kicks it. There is a long pause while he roams around belching.*)

Trammel up hmmm?
A-a-h the consequence and catch
(*A distant bell chimes.*)
WITH HIS SURCEASE! ! ! !
(*A bag of soot falls on his head.*)
successsss (*in a tiny whisper. A cannon goes off.*)

Fortunately, the poor quality of most Coarse Actors means a director need not worry himself too much about this sort of thing. Moves and business should be kept as simple as possible. An audience will have much more fun from unrehearsed crises, such as when the sofa collapses.

At some point a person calling itself the set designer will appear. Have nothing to do with them. Whatever conception the director has of the play, the designer somehow takes a different view.

Some years ago I played in a production of *Lear* in which the director said he considered Lear was a man trapped in a tube; the designer saw him lost in a symbolic wilderness. They never did get together. The director gave us all tiny movements with Lear huddled up in corners like a foetus; the designer burst forth with a great open stage, relieved only by a vast phallic symbol in the middle.

A Coarse director is prepared for this and keeps up his sleeve one or two wheezes for overcoming the hostility of the designer. If the director of Lear had been wise he would have had some stage rocks constructed secretly to fill up the open space. However, if you are the sort of person who considers Lear is stuck in a tube. I suppose such devices are above you.

Most Coarse Actors have little idea of their whereabouts on the stage so a director may have some trouble with masking. There is a simple way of avoiding this. Do not tell the offending actor to move, as he will merely shuffle in front of someone else. Simply say to the actor who is being masked, 'Harry, Fred is masking you.' Harry will immediately remedy the situation himself.

Coarse Actors are also very gregarious. Unless watched they always huddle in groups on stage, or else get in a ghastly straight line.

At an early stage in the rehearsal period a director should make a careful note of all the psychotics in the cast and weed them out. This is probably his most important task. (Psychotics include gripers, moaners, weirdies and people who are always being ill.)

Some of this type can be spotted at once, such as the man who misses the first rehearsal with an excuse about having had a fainting fit. Unless checked immediately he will appear spasmodically then vanish altogether a week before the opening night. Have him out at once.

Watkins played with one psycho who vanished for a fortnight just before the show and then had the cheek to turn up on the first night after somebody else had been called in to replace him. They had a great row in the dressing-room, both of them fighting to get into the same costume until each grabbed one leg of a pair of tights and pulled until they came in half.

I would include know-alls among the psychotics. If any person comes to a director after the first reading and starts offering advice and comment – have him out. This sort of person causes endless trouble in rehearsal, holding everyone up for hours to discuss futile points of interpretation of one word. In the dressing-room he advises everyone on what to do and then comes on without a vital prop.

A war play gives the greatest opportunity for the know-alls. Baron Munchausen would give up at the lies the cast will tell about their service experience. Askew and I were in a production of one of the many plays spawned by National Service. It collapsed in chaos because everyone insisted on drilling in their own way ('And I'm telling you that in the RAF we gave the command on the left foot . . .'). On the first night a complete squad of soldiers crashed into the scenery because everyone had a different version of the drill.

The message is plain. Evict all 'experts' from the cast, especially drill experts.

Another important task early in rehearsal is for the director to pave the way for his disappearance, in case the problems are too much. He or she should quietly drop hints about a possible business trip abroad ('My God, I hope they don't send me to Sweden just when I'm getting to grips with the production . . .'). This excuse can be activated when you can't face any more.

As rehearsals progress the inevitable difficulty will arise of the cast's slowness to learn lines. A simple way of encouraging them is to threaten to cut any speech that is not known.

Pretend this is being done as a favour to the actor.

'OK, Charlie, that's obviously a difficult speech and perhaps a bit too much, hmmmm? Just cut it altogether.'

By some miracle the actor usually learns the speech in the next ten minutes.

But be careful if you have any of the Method school in the cast. I knew an earnest young disciple who had one line in a play. They cut this line at the first rehearsal, but every time we came to that spot a spasm used to flit over his face.

When asked what the trouble was he replied, 'I've got the thought, but not the line.'

In the end they had to put the line back.

A further problem for the director is that all actors love being maimed and wounded. I have already told how all Coarse armies limp. It is reputed that as a child Askew wrecked the school Nativity play by portraying Joseph as a deformed cripple. I remember a director in later years trying to insist to Askew that there was no historical evidence that Julius Caesar had a club foot.

I was in *Oh, What a Lovely War* not long ago and was cast in the scene where the wounded soldiers arrive at Waterloo. The first rehearsal will live long in my mind as the soldier's injuries grew and grew. 'Please may I be blind?' we all chorused at the director. Those who weren't allowed to be blind were jealous and compensated by asking, 'Would it be a good idea if I had one leg/arm? I sort of feel I've been wounded in the groin . . . can I have a crutch?' By the end of rehearsal the room was filled with limping, hobbling, bandaged, gibbering wrecks, hanging on to each other and falling down at every chance.

Female Coarse Actors usually have the opposite syndrome. They insist on being beautiful whatever the occasion. You see them in *Mother Courage* carefully arranging their hair in the dressing-room to look pretty.

Rehearsals up to the dress rehearsal will be mostly a waste

of time, except for helping the cast to learn lines and moves. In fact, all that is achieved by any rehearsal not on stage is to train the cast in wrong ways, e.g. going out of exits which do not exist, or where the orchestra will be.

Whatever takes place at the dress rehearsal will bear absolutely no relation to what has gone before. The first thing to be discovered is that the set is completely different from the plan used in rehearsal. Probably the designer has omitted a door, so all the exits and entrances go for nothing and the whole show has to be plotted again.

Even if the set does have the requisite number of doors it is probable that one of them will open on to a brick wall. One might think this would only happen with a hired hall, but in fact it is just as likely to occur in a theatre which the designer has known for years. Sets are not designed for acting in, but as exercises in artistry.

The set will not fit the stage. Law Five states: 'All Coarse Acting sets are designed to be six inches bigger than the maximum possible size.'

The furniture will be at least four times as big as that used in rehearsal. Property mistresses must scour the junk shops of the world for the elephantine pieces they produce. Usually, when all furniture and props are set there is no room for anything else (and that includes the actors). All doors are firmly blocked.

Anything other than speaking or squeezing between the furniture will be found impossible. The drink of whisky which was so important to the plot cannot be managed now, because to reach the sideboard it is necessary to climb over the sofa which in turn is blocking the door through which the man who drinks the whisky has to enter. The fight scene has to be cut.

To make matters worse, the rehearsal will have to continue with men and women in overalls crawling like flies around the stage. I do not know why it is, but set painters, electricians, sound engineers and so forth do nothing for six weeks while rehearsals are going on and then suddenly spring to life just as the dress rehearsal starts.

Also, all sorts of strange people who normally are never seen crawl out of little holes and make their presence felt. I was present at one dress rehearsal where a man started to mend the roof with a hammer just as the curtain rose.

Forget the old theatrical tag about a bad dress rehearsal usually preceding a good first night. A bad dress rehearsal usually means a bad first night – and a bad second night, come to that. In fact at the dress rehearsal the Coarse director is face to face with the stark truth.

Tell the cast just how bad they are without mincing words. Besides, this will be the last chance to give them a torrent of abuse, so let them have it for all it's worth. Don't worry about depressing the cast – a depressed cast is a good cast, especially in comedies. The amount of laughter from the audience is usually in inverse ratio to the enjoyment of the cast. Ideally they should be nervous, sweating, depressed and worn-out. The finest performance I ever saw was from a man who got sacked from his job just as he left the office to go on stage.

Why not carry this idea further and approach the leading man with imaginary bad news just before the curtain rises. Clap him on the shoulder and say urgently, 'Listen, Harry, I don't want to upset you before you go on, but we've just had a phone message for you. No, I won't tell you now, in case it affects your performance. Just forget it and go on there and kill 'em.'

Whatever happens, a wheeze like that will effectively stop any tendency to laughter and giggling on stage, and if a director can achieve that with Coarse Actors he has certainly accomplished something.

Incidentally, don't let the cast see a programme at the dress rehearsal. The list of misspelt names and grammatical and factual errors will merely infuriate them.

Although one may insult actors as much as one likes, never be vituperative to stage staff. Despite the fact that they have sat on their backsides for six weeks while everyone else has been rehearsing, with the result that the sound effects don't work, the lighting looks as if a thunderstorm is going on and the set wouldn't fit Covent Garden, you must not upset them. They go sullen and threaten to strike. I know, I've done back-stage work myself, and I don't know a more recalcitrant, touchy and slow-moving scene-shifter. One can't help it – a strange sense of resentment creeps over you.

Eventually the first night will arrive. The director's final job before the curtain goes up is to arrange the order in which the cast is to change round in case of illness or non-arrival of an actor, and if necessary to arrange for substitutes to stand by. He himself will already have learned a smattering of everyone's part.

This routine must be kept up right to the final performance. I remember a production of my own in which I sat happily watching the last night. All my troubles seemed over and I was almost enjoying it for once when there was an uneasy pause in Act Two. I dashed back stage to find that one of the actors hadn't turned up. While the cast fluffed their way through we telephoned his home.

'I thought the show finished last night,' he explained plaintively. Seizing a copy of the script, the stage manager and I there and then rewrote the play to cut out every one of his subsequent entrances. But somehow the rest of the play seemed to lack something.

A Coarse director can never count himself at ease until the curtain has fallen on the final performance, and even then there may be some unpleasant legacy to deal with, such as the ruining of the costumes or the fact that the society tried to dodge paying royalties.

Don't forget to have a word with the stage manager before the curtain rises. My publishers will not allow me to print the word, but have it all the same.

Some directors break all the unwritten laws of the Theatre and spend the performance back stage, giving instructions to the cast and stage staff and throwing everything into confusion. The first time I met one of this type was a severe shock. I was in the middle of a speech when a rasping voice from the wings ground out 'Pep it up, old man' and I turned to see the angry red face of the director peering at me over the prompt's shoulder. It completely unnerved me.

I don't, however, suggest that a Coarse director should sit in the auditorium right through the show. The strain would be too great. Personally I always go over to the pub as soon as the first actor dries. This means I am in there by about seven-thirty-five. Return at the first interval, and it is surprising how much better the show will look.

Never go on stage afterwards for a curtain call, even if called for by the audience. People will only say it was all rigged. Besides, immediately the curtain has fallen it is your duty to seek out the representative of the local Press and ply him with drink.

Then go back stage and congratulate the cast. Don't tell the truth. Thank them. Finally invite a chosen few round to your home for drinks. The idea of this is to stir up jealousy and ensure a few friends in the society for future occasions. After the production most of the cast are going to be enemies anyway, so try to save something from the wreck by picking a few chosen cronies to stand by you.

And if the day has been a bad one comfort yourself as you crawl into bed with the unfortunate experience of a man who was once directing Dame Edith Evans. After rehearsal had been on for half an hour, during which he had made several ineffectual interruptions, she turned, fixed her eyes on him and said loudly, 'Who is this person?'

At least nobody has been *that* crushing.

APPENDIX TO CHAPTER SIX

Suggested time-table for an amateur production taking place on April 1:

Jan. 1 – Feb. 1: Cast play secretly.

Feb. 3: Formal reading for parts. Results ignored.

Feb. 5: Issue rehearsal schedule.

Feb. 7: Production conference. Discover designer plans to do whole thing with a Z-shaped stage.

Feb. 8: Resignation of set designer.

Feb. 10: Anonymous insulting phone call received.

Feb. 11: Further insulting phone call received. Believed to emanate from aggrieved actor.

Feb. 12: Set designer calls at home and drinks all the gin. Very penitent. Sorry he called you a stupid, ignorant philistine. Now wants to do play on L-shaped stage.

Feb. 13: Set designer resigns for second time.

Feb. 14: Insulting Valentine, with obscene overtones, received from unknown source.

Feb. 15: First rehearsal. Half cast absent. Copies of play apparently not available in Europe.

Feb. 16: Blocking rehearsal. Cancelled after half an hour as no one knows what the set will look like.

Feb. 17: Three characters drop out.

Feb. 20: Conference with new set designer, who wishes to perform the play on a 'womb-shaped stage'.

Feb. 22: Resignation of new set designer.

Feb. 24: Leading man announces he cannot attend any more rehearsals on Mondays, Wednesdays and Fridays.

Feb. 27: Approached by original set designer, who is willing to concede that play can be done on a conventional stage.

March 1: Leading lady says she cannot attend rehearsals on Tuesdays, Thursdays and Sundays.

March 3: Stage manager appears for first time.

March 5: Further insulting message received.

March 7: Treasurer of society says he is very worried about the amount of money being spent on set, costumes and lights. He only got to hear of it when Strand Electric rang up to ask when they wanted to take delivery of the back-projection equipment. Five skips of satin costumes have also been delivered, together with ninety feet of timber and half a dozen twelve-foot flats.

March 8: Rehearsals cancelled for three days for long conferences with wardrobe, lighting department and set designer.

March 10: Resignation of wardrobe, lighting staff and set designer.

March 11: Treasurer on phone to ask for explanation of large crate which has arrived. Dare not open it as he intends to send it back immediately.

March 12: Stage manager vanishes, taking book with him.

March 13: Scripts now available.

March 14: Wardrobe mistress arrives in tears and starts sewing again.

March 15: Angry complaint from curator, stating that every time a crate of china is delivered at the Memorial Hall someone sends it straight back again. Passed to treasurer.

March 17: Set designer reappears as if nothing had happened.

March 19: Further insulting phone call received.

March 20: Four minor characters drop out.

March 21: Reporter sees cast, writes advance piece for local paper, with special reference to leading man.

March 24: Leading man drops out.

March 25: Leading man replaced.

March 26: Leading man offers to return. Refused.

March 28: Attempt to hold run-through in hall ruined by sound operator with tape-recorder who insists on playing it backwards for hours on end. When asked why he could not have done this earlier he disappears, taking the club tape-recorder with him.

March 29: DRESS REHEARSAL: No costumes, set or props available.

March 31: FINAL DRESS REHEARSAL: Discover set designer has not allowed for any exits, and forestage obliterates two rows of stalls. New lighting man arrives and fuses all lights halfway through first act. Play is re-plotted hastily to allow for sofa which is so big that it hangs over the footlights. Finish 1 a.m. Leading lady then throws hysterics, complaining someone is using her mirror. Home 2.45 a.m.

April 1: FIRST NIGHT: Insulting telegram waiting at hall. Just before curtain rises notice there is something odd about the way the chairs are arranged and discover that box office are working to the original stage plan, with the result that there is a Z-shaped gap in the audience. After three minutes observe flat is teetering and cannot stand suspense, so leave auditorium to pace up and down outside. Great shout of laughter announces collapse of flat. Buoyed up by many congratulations after show, then depressed by former leading man, who says he thought everyone *tried* hard. Overhear conversation in toilets in which two people are saying what they *really* thought of the play. Bitterly depressed. Drown sorrows.

April 4: Read local paper account. 'Hard-working cast . . . very funny situations . . . slick business . . . bore comparison with West End standards . . . brilliantly directed . . .'

April 5: Suggest to committee that might be willing to tackle another production next year, if can spare time, etc., etc.

7 The Open-air

'Warble his native wood notes wild . . .' MILTON

The prompt which reached Southend – Unpleasantness on the roof of a public convenience – when Maureen sank – difficulty of playing in fog – when your crown turns to wet cardboard

Law Six of Coarse Drama states that on the performance of any play in the open-air:

1. An immense flock of screeching birds with loose bowels will fly to and fro over the audience and the stage.
2. The Air Traffic Controller at London Airport will immediately re-route seventy-five jet airliners over the acting area.
3. A brass band nearby will start to play 'Poet and Peasant' fortissimo, preferably when someone on stage is dying.
4. Five motor-cars will crash noisily in the vicinity, with a screeching of tyres.
5. Rain, fog and tempest will descend without warning.

Yet despite all this there are still brave souls who like acting in the open-air, and those who like watching, and even I have a soft spot for it myself, despite my criticisms.

A director in charge of such a show must first of all realize that no one in the audience is going to hear more than half of what is said. Even so, avoid the temptation to employ microphones and amplifiers.

If these are used it will be found that they are of a special type, issued only to amateur dramatic societies, which pick up nothing but the noise of the wind. While the actors are

84

mouthing hopelessly all the audience will hear is a scratchy booming sound, with an occasional ear-splitting electronic shriek.

The only time I knew a loudspeaker to work was when the prompt used it. She was ingeniously tucked away behind a bush, since there was nowhere else to hide her. A speaker was concealed in a tree and she was supposed to whisper any prompt into the microphone. Our electrician assured us the speaker was adjusted to be quiet yet audible to the cast.

The first prompt could have been heard at Southend (the show was in the Midlands). In fact Petruchio, who was leaning against the tree containing the speaker, leaped two feet in the air when he heard it. Worse, the wretched microphone was so sensitive that it picked up every rustle from the prompter's clothing, so the first half was punctuated by mysterious crackling noises and breathing sounds, until we rescued the poor girl at the interval.

Another of the difficulties over audibility is that more people will be watching the show from outside the auditorium, than from inside. (LAW SEVEN OF COARSE DRAMA: 'Every open-air production is sited near a public convenience with a flat roof, which will be crammed with juvenile delinquents.')

Since these people feel themselves free to make as much noise as they like, and even to criticize the show loudly, the noise level is considerably higher than in a normal theatre.

An attempt to salvage something from this by taking the collecting box round will be met with insulting words. As a child at the seaside I remember a concert party on the sands who used to send the chief comic round on an expedition to clear the children off their free perch on top of the public lavatory ('Go on, Charlie, hop round and get them kids off the urinal'). But somehow I don't see this working with an amateur group.

Fortunately, and this is a point in favour of open-air acting, the very dampening effect that the open-air has on an actor's voice works in the opposite direction, so that the players are blissfully ignorant of the chaos and bedlam in front of them, and that their carefully rehearsed speeches are vanishing somewhere around the third row of the stalls.

Against this is the fact that the actors can see the audience.

It is really depressing to watch people stand up and file out in the middle of one's long speech. And the audience are much more easily distracted than in an indoor theatre. My best speech at the Minack cliff-top theatre, Cornwall, was ruined by the launching of the local lifeboat. Actors can't compete with real-life drama.

Whereas in an indoor production the setting can be adapted to fit the play, in an outdoor show the play has to be adapted to fit the setting, and the director must remember this. I say remember it, but then immediately forget it.

It might seem very nice in theory to have Caliban swing from the branches of a real tree like a gorilla, but in practice either the branch will break or the park-keeper will chop off the only suitable branch just before the performance.

Askew's sister Maureen had an unhappy experience while playing Ariel. The director wished to make use of a very pretty lake which framed the acting area, and had placed, a few inches under the water, a series of concrete blocks, so that Ariel could appear to tiptoe over the water.

Unfortunately, a child in a paddle-boat, finding his navigational rights obstructed in this way, moved a block to one side, with the result that Maureen vanished up to her thighs in mud with a fearful screech.

That was a production which had everything a director should avoid, including a live horse, which fertilized the stage while someone was seated on it, making a speech. There was also an orchestra on a floating platform at the side of the lake. I should like to say that the platform sank, but the worst that happened was that the mooring became untied and it drifted slowly out to the middle, gradually turning round so that the orchestra had their backs to the audience.

In addition, one of the small-part players had the unfortunate habit of rushing across the park to a public house in full costume and make-up during the show, with the result that a crocodile of children used to follow him about, and stand outside the saloon bar, chattering and pointing at him.

I suppose the greatest experience of the open-air theatre is the pageant, not least because of the cast of thousands, most of whom are Coarse Actors of the vilest kind, malevolent children, sulky teenagers and incompetent housewives. There seems to be a sort of standard form of acting for pageants, in which nobody pays any attention to the principals or the plot and carries on as suits them best. A man who played in his borough pageant told me that when he was Simon de Montfort addressing the serfs he noticed that every single serf had his back to him. They were looking at their friends in the audience.

The impression of Coarse acting on an enormous scale is heightened by the futility of the dialogue, which is probably composed by a local headmaster:

Enter a thane clutching his stomach

SECOND THANE: Art thou wounded, Olaff?
FIRST THANE: Nay, 'tis but a scratch. But tell the King we must away . . .

An experienced open-air director will *never* make alternative arrangements to perform indoors if the weather is bad.

The mere fact of going to the trouble of making such arrangements seems to ensure a supply of freak storms and depressions. The whole of a director's day is one long worry as he glances at the clouds every five minutes wondering whether to ring up the stage manager and tell her to put all the chairs in the hall, and finally about five o'clock, as the heavens open, he makes his decision and teams of sweating stage-hands transfer the whole production into the hall or marquee.

As they are carrying in the last chair a blast of heat strikes them, sunshine of a hitherto unheard-of intensity floods the park and a rainbow glows mockingly over the deserted acting area.

I remember fog threatening a production at the lovely open-air theatre at Torquay (alas, no more). We hastily moved indoors, and, sure enough, by the interval the place was like an oven.

It was so hot that we moved outside again, whereupon a dense mist rolled up from the sea and enveloped everything in gloom, through which the occasional line could be heard filtering.

Sooner or later in the show the director will be faced with the most awful decision of all. Do we go on through this downpour, or do we stop now?

I have played with the press-on-at-all-costs type who insist on continuing, with the remnants of the audience huddled under trees and peering furtively from their umbrellas, while the actors' costumes cling soggily to the skin and the cardboard spears begin to fall apart. And I have played under the timid directors who call it all off at the merest hint of a shower, while the audience sit in their shirt-sleeves and grow restive.

Personally I would say press on. People may not appreciate the acting but they do admire the courage, and while they may not stay to see the show finish, at least they will have a word of praise for the cast when they return home ('I don't know how they stuck it in all that rain. And that poor King, with all the gold paint running off his crown . . .').

In fact it will probably be the only time in a Coarse Actor's life that he will receive the genuine and unstinted admiration of the audience. The fact that all the costumes will be ruined will be a small price to pay.

8 The Stage Manager and Back-stage Staff

'I'll come no more behind your scenes, David; for the silk stockings and white bosoms of your actresses excite my amorous propensities . . .'
DR JOHNSON

Importance of stage manager in wrecking production – stage manager need not remain unseen – how to blow up the theatre – all-purpose Coarse costume – Unpleasantness with a property club – collapse of elderly director – *The Rivals* on wheels

It is a perpetual subject for debate as to whether the stage manager and his team of slow-witted malcontents are responsible for ruining more productions than the actors. On the whole the actors probably take the honour by a short head, because the stage manager by virtue of his work must normally remain unseen by the audience.

The fact, however, that a stage manager is not seen by the audience does not mean that he cannot impose his personality on a play as much as an actor or director. Inside every stage manager there is an actor trying to get out and the true Coarse stage manager will study means and ways of satisfying his histrionic desires.

I say that an SM's work means that he must remain invisible, but this is not always so. There have been frequent occasions on which stage managers have appeared in full view of the audience, to everyone's mutual delight.

There was, for instance, the occasion in London where the designer had the brilliant idea of cutting the set down to three pieces of mobile scenery. Each piece consisted of three flats fixed together to form a hollow triangle on tiny wheels, and in the middle of this stood an operator, hidden from the audience, wheeling the scenery about as the action demanded.

The play (the plot of which, I am afraid, rather eluded me) had many changes of scene, all taking place in Egypt some five thousand years ago. The effect was most impressive as the blind monoliths buzzed about the stage, now clustering to represent a grove of trees, now lined up to act as a city wall.

Unfortunately, one of the triangle operators was myself, and on the second night, after a triumphant opening performance, I was rather slow wheeling off at the end of a scene, and found myself stranded on stage in a black-out (there were no curtains).

I'm afraid I panicked. The audience rustled as they saw a tall, dim shape, with one wheel squeaking slightly, rushing all over the stage in the half-light. I made one dart to where I imagined the wings to be and was rewarded by a horrified shriek from the stalls. Apparently I pulled up six inches from the edge of the stage while the front row abandoned their seats. Eventually, with all sense of direction lost, I twirled miserably centre stage hoping for something to happen.

It was then that I became aware of someone knocking on the outside of my triangle and a voice called urgently: 'Mike, Mike. Are you there?'

It was the stage manager. I shouted 'Yes' in a voice that could have been heard all over the hall and he replied, 'I'll get you out of this, matey.'

Guiding me with a torch, he led me off stage, rather in the manner of someone helping an elderly lady through a fog, and released me from the wretched triangle.

Later we discovered that the black-out had lasted two minutes. The front row of the audience never did return.

Of course, that is only one example of a stage manager appearing to the audience. There are many others, such as the time at Northampton when a flat fell down to reveal the stage manager glued to the back of it. Apparently he had been trying to hold the two flats together by the well-known Coarse method of The Human Cleat and his weight overbalanced them.

There is no need for an SM to be ashamed of wishing to appear to the audience. He should wear a gaily-coloured (preferably fluorescent) sweater, so that if his arm has to appear round the edge of a flat, to replace a fallen prop, for instance, the audience will be in no doubt as to whose arm it is. Personally when stage-managing, I always have my initials embroidered on my arm, just in case. It is most gratifying to hear from the movement in the auditorium that your arm has not only been seen but has been recognized.

I have, in fact, known an SM and his helpers remain on-stage for a whole scene. It happened in a production of an operatic society where they were supposed to transform the setting swiftly during a black-out. They took so long the conductor started up the music, the lights went up and the cast came on. Meanwhile the stage management toiled on, trying to get sofas through tiny doors and hang a huge chandelier, as *The Merry Widow* thundered on all round them. The actors won by a short head and actually finished the scene before the stage hands had finished setting it. 'It's all go with this bloody lot,' said the stage manager afterwards.

The true Coarse stage manager regards the mechanics of his job, such as calling the actors, exerting back-stage discipline, etc., etc., as mere details, to be left to the unimaginative assistant stage managers. He will be more concerned with the artistic side, such as inventing a set of lies for the local authority about the fire precautions, and seeing that there are plenty of *empty* fire extinguishers lying about. Remember that full fire extinguishers are dangerous, as they may go off at an awkward moment.

Both in rehearsal and during the show he will be expected to deal with awkward callers, for the mere fact that a show is being performed seems to attract a string of strange persons to the hall. My friend Askew tells me of the time that a Water Board man was found wandering behind the scenery in *The Three Sisters* and had already been glimpsed through the window, to the mystification of the audience.

It is worth while for a stage manager to check that the performance is taking place in the correct hall. This is the sort of precaution which an inexperienced person would not bother with, but a Coarse stage manager never trusts anyone, least of all the secretary of the society.

If you have ever had the mortification of actually starting a performance, only to find that you are entertaining the wrong body of people in the wrong place, you will understand what

I mean. It really is astonishing what little difference it makes to the audience. In this instance they were apparently expecting a choir, and when we came on and started *Mother Courage* they were perfectly happy, until the choir arrived half an hour later and tried to come on stage as well.

CUEING. This is a most important subject. In the Coarse theatre there is only one certain means of cueing back stage, and that is for the stage manager to walk up behind the person receiving the cue and to hit him on the head when he has to begin.

How many times has one seen a lighting man staring at a winking cue light, mesmerized into inactivity? I know one SM who was so upset with the failure of his cue lights that he tied a piece of string to the wrists of the lighting and sound people, the idea being that when required he would pull the string. I have seen this recommended in several books.

The only result was that when he pulled the string the first time there was a long pause, and then just as all the lights should have gone out the lighting man appeared and said, 'Yes, did you want me?'

SOUND EFFECTS. Most sound effects are taped these days, of course, which has spoiled what used to be regarded as the highlight of the stage manager's evening. Sometimes the actors were called in to help. In *Henry V* we simulated the noise of battle off-stage by banging tin plates and mugs together while everyone went 'Urrgh, aah, blurch' etc. It sounded like someone eating a six-course meal and belching all the time.

But the use of recorded sound doesn't mean that the quality of effects on the Coarse stage is any better. It merely gives more opportunities for something to go wrong. If an effect can be produced live it is better to do it that way. Tapes have a built-in resistance to amateur dramatic societies. The actor is usually left saying 'Hark, I hear the sound of horses' hooves' in complete silence, and on looking off stage sees the effects operator enmeshed in yards of tape. Recorded trumpets are especially prone to faults. They have a habit of being late on cue so that the King enters in silence, yet every time he opens his mouth to speak there is a fanfare. And recorded fanfares *always* being with a strange wheeze, a sort of y-o-o-o-o-p that is most unregal.

At least with live sound one avoids the sort of Unpleasantness that occurred at Ealing in *Henry V*. The King made a suitably regal entrance and the heralds raised their fake trumpets when there burst from the loudspeakers not a fanfare but the sound of a battle going on.

I sometimes feel nostalgic for the days when nearly all sound effects were produced live by the stage manager. It was sheer bliss to work the wind machine with the thunder sheet going full blast and someone madly rolling dried peas on a drum beside you (for younger readers, that's how we used to imitate a storm). It was especially interesting to see the expressions on the actors' faces when you kicked up such a noise you drowned them. It is still worthwhile doing effects live where possible, as this gives a Coarse stage manager a chance to make his mark on the production, perhaps by adding unexpected noises. What is wrong with a little thunder in the middle of *The Cherry Orchard*?

It is strange how producing sound effects brings out aggression. Sound operators, with their tape recorders and amplifiers, must be watched stringently. Left to themselves they will obliterate any show.

I once played in a production of *Oh, What A Lovely War* in which the battle effects were in the hands of an audio-maniac, who was not content with the odd whine and crump in the background, but continually interrupted each speech with great moans, thuds, rat-a-tats and an obscure sound rather like an old bus exploding, which he said was the exact noise made by an three-inch mortar. The actors never had a chance. So don't blame me if your production is taken over by a little man in the sound-box. You have been warned.

By the way, if an actor has to play a musical instrument on stage do not allow him to play it himself or he may become so wrapped up that he will go on and on. My friend Askew once had to play a few bars of *The Moonlight Sonata* and very nearly went through the whole piece. He was in tears by the time he stopped.

I confess to having a personal interest in the production of

THE HUMAN CLEAT

USEFUL SOUND EFFECT
noise of cup dropping

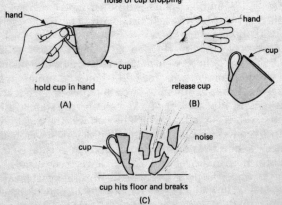

hold cup in hand

(A)

release cup

(B)

cup hits floor and breaks

(C)

stage effects, since I once wrote a book about it. It was the funniest book I have ever written and contained this gem: 'To make a noise like a tray of crockery being dropped, fill a tray full of broken crockery and drop it.' I only wish I could write stuff like that these days.

However, it seemed to fill a need, because several people wrote to me and said how helpful the book was. There was also a letter from a man who complained that in following my advice on how to produce a realistic air raid he set fire to the theatre.

Lovers of the Coarse Theatre may be interested to know how he did it. He strictly followed my instructions that maroons should be exploded in a dustbin, for safety's sake, but he forgot to tell his ASM what the dustbin was for, with the result that the dear girl filled it with wastepaper shortly before he let off the maroon. Not only was there a splendid blaze but members of the cast were showered with burning paper.

Crowd effects are an important part of the stage manager's task. Remember to keep exhibitionists out of an off-stage crowd. It is better to have a few stage-hands murmuring 'Rhubarb' than to have a lot of would-be actors making up strange lines of dialogue.

The people to avoid are those who regard shouting off stage as an excuse for delivering an unseen diatribe of their own invention ('Come on, lads, what are we waiting for, let's get in there and finish off Brutus and all that gang of filthy murderers. . . .'). It is most embarrassing if the crowd noise drops and drivel like that can be heard booming across the stage.

Some useful all-purpose Coarse sound-effects are described in the diagrams on page 94.

PROMPTING. This subject has been dealt with to some extent in the section on acting. From the stage management point of view it is important to treat the prompter as if she or he does not exist. Generally, of all the thousands of prompts delivered on the amateur stage each year, only about thirty per cent are given by the prompters. The rest come either from the cast or from the wise stage manager, snooping behind the scenery with the book in his hand, while the prompter nods to itself sagely and dreams of some furtive romance with the assistant electrician.

LIGHTING. The lighting department shares with the wardrobe and the sound-effects team the view that the show exists simply for their benefit. In the same way as the wardrobe mistress regards *The Miser* as an excuse for some nice frills and furbelows, so the lighting man looks at *St Joan* as merely an opportunity for some interesting flame effects.

A lighting man is not concerned with lighting either the actors or the set, but with lighting the lights, so that people will say, 'What wonderful lighting.'

Sometimes such praiseworthy adventure is restricted by lack of money. There are two ways of overcoming this:

1. Without any authority from the treasurer write to the Strand Electric Co. and hire everything under the sun from back projection equipment to pageant lamps. Then resign.

2. Keep the stage dark.

The second is the wiser course. These days, in the same way as nobody cares whether one can hear an actor, as long as you can distinguish the sound of him scratching his armpits, so nobody cares whether they *see* him or not. It is considered extremely modish if every scene takes place in utter gloom. By a strange paradox, the less light there is, the more the audience are inclined to praise the lighting staff for their cleverness.

If anyone protests, fob them off with a stream of meaningless technical drivel, such as: 'Listen, mate, a single-valvular, double thynamic board of this sort won't take any more than five hundred ohms linked in series-parallel. If I put any more on it I'll blow up the hall.'

As with all backstage departments, lighting are liable to do things which are totally opposed to what is happening on stage. Askew recalls a production of *Macbeth* in which the lighting controller insisted on shining a pink spot on the ghost of Banquo. He refused all appeals from the director. 'I think it looks nice,' he said.

Storms and effects generally often cause trouble in the lighting department, not so much because they go wrong (which is to be expected) but because the lighting section cannot stand competition. If there is a lighting and a sound effect going on at the same time a macabre race may develop.

There was a production of André Obey's *Noah* where a little gentle thunder and rain, together with spasmodic lightning, were called for. It all started well enough, with occasional rumbles in the background, and the odd flash, but gradually the audience became aware that the rumbles were growing in intensity and as they did so the lightning flashes grew more frequent and spectacular. Finally nothing could be heard or seen in the theatre but booming thunder-claps and blinding lights.

New societies would be well advised to use only a genuinely experienced person in charge of their lighting. Under no circumstances have anything to do with the man who says he knows a little about it, or any pamphlet entitled 'How to Make your own Lighting Installations'.

Watkins, who is a schoolmaster, found a do-it-yourself lighting expert from the sixth form sticking a six-inch nail in the blackened hole where the fuse had been, with the result that the third act was ruined by a stench of burning rubber and clouds of evil smoke which crept in from the wings. By the time the curtain call came there were only ten people left in the audience, and they were all clustered near the doors.

WARDROBE AND COSTUME. Another department whose influence is out of all proportion is the wardrobe. For practical purposes, many Coarse shows are directed by the wardrobe mistress.

For instance, it is useless for the director to say he wishes to set a play in a certain period. He may, for instance, want to try a Shakespearean production in eighteenth-century dress and he may key the whole manner of playing to that end, but if the wardrobe mistress happens to have a lot of Victorian junk lying around at the moment the production will finish up in the style of Prince Albert.

It is no use explaining the subtleties of dramatic production to a Coarse wardrobe mistress, any more than one can tell anything to the lighting man.

'Well, I think Hamlet would look very nice in that shirt

John wore as Disraeli,' they say when you try to explain that Hamlet is to be dressed as an army officer of 1750. And whatever arguments the director puts forward, Disraeli's shirt will make its appearance in the end. Personally, I always go to wardrobe before I even plot a play, and say, 'What period would you like it in?' It saves a lot of trouble.

This assumes that the wardrobe department allow you to produce the play of your choice. In my experience, often they won't. If a society chooses a Molière, or anything that needs a lot of costume, they'll say it can't be done, why don't we do something simpler such as *The Caretaker*? And they always get their way. It is easier, when planning the year's programme, to go to wardrobe and ask what costumes they have got.

Law Eight of Coarse Drama is that all garments designed and made by a company's own staff are for being photographed in and not acting in.

I shall always remember my costume for a small part in *Othello*. It was set in a vague period which I shall call all-purpose Coarse Renaissance. My costume, however, looked like something from the Battle of Hastings. The bottom half consisted of baggy trousers such as women wear in a Turkish harem, with some tapes would round. The upper part was simply a long cylinder.

It was all very puzzling, so I went to the wardrobe mistress and I said: 'Look, this cylinder thing. Are you sure it's not part of the set?' She was very insulted, so I simply put my legs through two holes at the bottom of the cylinder, pulled it up to the chin and held it there with string.

When I walked on stage for the costume parade the designer had hysterics.

'No, no, no, Michael,' she screamed. 'It's upside down. You put your *arms* through the two holes, not your legs. You've ruined the whole effect.'

However, when I put it on the right way I found I couldn't move. My sword fight was like a marionette dance. So after the dress rehearsal I wore the wretched thing upside down for the rest of the run and nobody complained at all.

But it is a *sine qua non* of the Coarse costume that it is impossible to move in it. Part of the reason for the poor standard of movement in amateur drama is, I am convinced, due to this. And if by some mischance the costume does allow one to move, then it will fall off at the slightest provocation.

Coarse costumes are invariably held together by the most primitive means. One would not believe that the zipper had been invented. A favourite method of fastening is to have one hook at the top of the costume and one eye at the bottom. These, of course, are at the back so that if one has a quick change in a deserted dressing-room it is impossible to do up even these primitive fastenings and one has to rush on stage with costume flapping wildly.

For the great mass of Coarse actors, such as Shakespearean spear-carriers, rustics, clowns, etc., a special all-purpose Coarse garment seems to have grown up by tradition. There is a photograph between pages 64 and 65.

This garment is suitable for: Old Gobbo, Young Gobbo, Pistol, Nym, Bardolph, French Prisoner, Messenger, Boatswain, Trinculo, Stephano, a Sea Captain, an Officer, Speed, Launce, Clown, Bottom, Snug, Flute, Snout, Quince, Starveling, Costard, a Forester, Adam, Dennis, Touchstone, Corin, Silvius, William, a Steward, Tranio, Biondella, Grumio, Curtis, Pedant, Christopher Sly, Autolycus, an Old Shepherd, Second Citizen of Angiers, Gaoler, Gadshill, Peto, Vintner, Drawer, First Ostler, Second Ostler, Davy, Mouldy, Shadow, Wart, Feeble, Bullcalf, Beadle, Groom, a French Sergeant, Son of the Master Gunner of Orleans, Corpse of King Henry V, Several Petitioners, a Son That Hath Killed His Father, a Father That Hath Killed His Son, First Murderer, Second Murderer, Doorkeeper to the Council Chamber, Thersites, Servant to Triolus, Servant to Paris, Servant to Diomedes, Flaminius, Lucilius, Servilius, Caphia, Philotus, Titus, Lucius, Hortensius, Two of Timon's creditors, a Citizen of Antium, a Soothsayer, another Poet, Varro, Clotius, Claudius, Strato, Lucius, Dardanius, Pindarus, First, Second, Third, Fourth and Fifth Citizens, Pisanio, a Dutch Gentleman, Philemon, Leonine, a Pander, Boult, Fishermen, King Lear, Sampson, Gregory, Peter, Abraham, an Apothecary, Musician, Bleeding Sergeant, Drunken Porter, Ghost of Banquo, Young Siward, First Grave-digger, Second Grave-digger, Player King, Fortinbras, Danish Captain, etc., etc., with apologies for any omissions.

The garment basically consists of a shapeless shroud, sometimes gathered in at the waist by a sword-belt, which will fall off at the slightest movement. The all-purpose garment is inevitably made of hessian, painted to the appropriate colour, so that an actor comes off stage covered in dye and suffering from a strange rash.

The nether parts of the all-purpose garment are tights, made of some special material which wrinkles and falls down no matter what precautions are taken. Coins twisted in the waist will delay the falling down for a few moments, but the only result is that the waist of the tights stretches until the circumference is about five feet. If braces are worn the offending tights stretch until they might comfortably fit a man twelve feet tall, and the waistband comes over your ears. In that case remember to cut two holes for the eyes. The crotch of this garment is always round the knees.

In addition, one foot of the Coarse tight faces one way, and the other in the opposite direction. I never know why this is.

There is an equivalent all-purpose garment for women, consisting of a kind of obscene shift, which is so designed that in moments of violence one bosom is liable to fall out of it.

There is also Coarse armour, consisting of thick string painted silver and knitted with telegraph poles by teams of ancient women. The legs of this are always drooping and full of holes, and if you can avoid wearing it do so. Since the wearing of armour means that you will either be killed or crowned, and it is impossible to do either with dignity when the trousers are coming down, revealing an old bathing costume underneath, it is better not to wear armour at all.

Class distinction exists in costume, too. Wardrobe will spend weeks of loving care on a few costumes for the principals and then throw rubbish at the Coarse players, male and female. Hence the wardrobe mistress who inspected a Shakespeare cast in their tights and then announced, 'Jockstraps will be issued free only to those with large parts.'

Finally, some warnings, First, never allow anyone to mend tights while you are wearing them, unless you are impervious to pain. In fact, never allow any garment to be mended while wearing it. Only recently I saw a terrible accident as a result of this advice being ignored when a wardrobe girl mended the dress of an actress while she was seated in a crowded dressing-room. When the actress rose to go on stage it was discovered she had been sewn to the girl next to her.

Another warning is: never lend anything to the wardrobe department. Apart from the fact that the costume will come back covered in make-up and with strange cigarette ends in all the pockets, the only thanks will be to hear people say 'Where did he get that dreadful coat?'

And worse can happen. A woman was approached by the producer of an impecunious amateur society who asked if he could borrow her velvet curtains for an eighteenth-century play. The good lady agreed and went to see the show. Her enjoyment was spoiled in the second act when the producer himself came on wearing a velvet suit which looked rather familiar. After some minutes she realized that it had been cut from her curtains.

Before leaving the subject of wardrobe, yet another warning must be issued: never wash your own costume.

I issue this injunction as a result of a performance of *A Midsummer Night's Dream* in which we wore extravagant costumes that had been hand-painted.

Midway through the run Titania boiled hers. It immediately turned grey and shrank to a tiny piece of material like a doll's knickers.

Since all costumes will be so constructed as to shrivel and fall apart at a touch, let wardrobe do the cleaning and take the blame. And if they do remove a costume for cleaning remember that what will return next night will bear little relation to what you have been wearing.

PROPERTIES. Properties are never available for the rehearsal of a Coarse play. It is impossible to obtain so much as a potato before the dress rehearsal.

I believe the reason is that the property department likes to spring little surprises upon the actors. They leave the unsuspecting creatures rehearsing for six weeks with a substitute property such as a toy pistol, and on the night produce a vast sort of blunderbuss which according to the script is supposed to be hidden in the waistcoat pocket.

Props are at their best over food. The actor mimes a

four-course meal in rehearsal, despatching it in three minutes, of which two and a half are taken up in dialogue. At the dress rehearsal props either provide a genuine four-course meal which holds up the play for twenty minutes, or else a plastic chicken which the unhappy actor has to beat at with his fork and say 'Yum, yum'.

On the whole, though, it is better to have the fake meal than the real thing. Apart from the fact that real fish and chips fill the theatre with a ghastly stench, the food is invariably cold. In a performance of James Saunders's one-act *Double Double*, which takes place in a bus canteen, I tried to tackle cold chips, cold fried cod in congealed fat, all covered in cold tomato sauce and washed down with cold tea. After three mouthfuls I felt so sick I had to leave the stage.

It was in the same production, by the way, that one actor claimed he found hot sausages and cold custard on his plate, while someone else was trying to eat apple pie and gravy.

Always make a point of inspecting personal props. It is not a bad idea secretly to blunt the swords and daggers of opponents, as props love to provide lethal instruments. Spears should be especially well scrutinized, as all Coarse spears have heads which fall off. Assume any cigarette lighter may not work, that the matches will be dead, and that the pistol will not fire.

Carefully test any liquid you have to drink on-stage, such as whisky, beer, tea or even lemonade. Make the first swig a cautious one. At the best, the liquid will be water, coloured with cold tea or cochineal. At the worst it may be positively poisonous, as when someone painted the inside of my silver papier-mâché mug and the paint came off when it was filled. It looked rather odd when I raised high my tankard in a toast and then spat all over the stage.

If cold tea is to be used, do not store it in an old whisky bottle. I say this as a result of a disastrous experience, when the props girl filled a teapot from an old whisky bottle she used to store her fake 'tea'. Unfortunately, it was a genuine bottle of whisky, the one the stage manager kept for a quick snort when he felt depressed. The resulting tea party on-stage was one of the most extraordinary things I've ever seen, with the cast taking great gulps of tea and then tottering about gasping for breath and calling for water.

SET DESIGN AND CONSTRUCTION. As stated earlier, sets are not designed to be acted upon, but are produced for the glory of the designer. As long as directors and actors know this they will save a lot of trouble and heart-burning. It is well known that sets cannot be painted until the curtain has gone up at the dress rehearsal, when a girl with a ladder will start to wander round the stage, spilling paint over everybody.

Yet Coarse designers will be well advised to remember the virtues of simplicity. It is possible for even a set to be laughed at. Some years ago there was a vogue (started at Stratford-on-Avon) for sets in two pieces, on wheels, which miraculously came together as the curtain rose, or slid apart at the end of a scene.

My friend Askew, who at that time was working in South Wales, tells me that during *The Rivals* half a house glided on stage without the other half appearing. Being of an inquisitive nature, Askew worked his way to the wings where he found the other half of the scenery inextricably jammed.

He returned and the scene continued. A few minutes later, feeling he ought to pretend that the whole thing was deliberate, he casually leaned against the end of the piece of scenery which had appeared, whereupon it glided silently into the wings, throwing him to the ground and leaving the stage bare.

SUMMARY. I cannot conclude this chapter without the most important warning of all: Never marry the ASM. This applies to both sexes.

9   Front of House and Organizations

'Sir, the gentlemen will be angry if you sit there . . .' The Malcontent (JOHN MARSTON)

Unpleasantness in the toilets – don't shoot the reporter, he's doing his best – regrettable outbreak of deafness – how not to get a cup of coffee

HOUSE MANAGER AND STEWARDS. One of the biggest joys for the true connoisseur of Coarse Drama is the activities of the front-of-house staff. It is remarkable that while the actors can hardly be heard the house staff all have booming, resonant voices which they do not hesitate to use during the performance. Frequently a scene will be ruined by this sort of dialogue:

'QUIET, PLEASE, THE PERFORMANCE HAS STARTED. MAY I SEE YOUR TICKET, MADAM? I SAID "MAY I SEE YOUR TICKET, MADAM?" AH, F6 AND F7? DOWN THE LEFT-HAND AISLE NEAR THE FRONT . . . JUST A MOMENT, SIR . . . .'

In many amateur societies it might be a good idea to exchange the front-of-house staff with the actors, thus ensuring that at least the cast will be audible.

The duties of a Coarse house manager have little in common with those of his equivalent in the professional theatre, who appears merely to stride about in evening dress with a flower stuck in the buttonhole, making himself pleasant to Sydney Bernstein or Kenneth Tynan if they should happen to look in.

A Coarse house manager will find himself busy dealing with the inevitable confusion of the box-office, the refreshment staff and the publicity. For instance, while the posters say the curtain will rise at eight, the tickets state seven-forty-five and the stage manager says seven-thirty (the local Press have the times right but the days wrong).

Many an actor has come on stage to find a half-empty house with people still pouring in from all directions. That, I suppose, is preferable to coming on to a completely empty house ('I'm sorry, old man, you distinctly told me that it would only run for three nights. How was I to know you were playing on Friday'). Although the ultimate horror is having an audience and no cast, a house manager's nightmare which only too often comes true.

In addition there is the Ninth Law of Coarse Drama to contend with. This states: 'On any given night of an amateur dramatic show there will be an overflow in the toilets.'

Far from wearing the traditional evening dress and flower, a house manager would be well advised to come in overalls and rubber waders, and bring a plumber's plunger with him.

Another hazard peculiar to all amateur drama is dealing with members of the audience who have gone to sleep. Amateur drama is bound to contain a higher percentage of unwilling attenders in the audience than professional shows, but these unwilling members of the audience, usually patient fathers, have a knack of consoling themselves with a couple of drinks beforehand and then dozing off noisily. Ideally, one should have a long pole and tap them gently on the head, but if this is impossible one will just have to find an excuse for asking loudly if they are in the right seats.

Drunk members of the audience are fortunately rare, although I recall an actor who was so piqued at not being cast in a show that he got plastered on the first night and interfered with the scene by saying loudly, 'Ha, ha, very funny,' at all the humorous lines. Fortunately he fell asleep for the rest of the first half and did not return after the interval.

As few amateur societies have a stage door the house manager will find himself having to deal with would-be visitors backstage. It is best to pretend to pass on a message but in fact don't do so, as a protection to the cast. How can someone do justice to a part when she gets a message: 'Your ex-husband is in the audience and asked me to tell you he will kill himself if you don't return.'

The house manager, like the stage manager, will be on

guard against a stream of interrupters, and will station himself at the main door to intercept them. These will range from the inevitable policeman ('Is the owner of 786 YMX here?') to drunken Irishmen trying to get in for the Shamrock Ball, and acting members of the society attempting to sneak in for nothing (actors always seem to be under the impression that they do not need to buy tickets). He will also be prepared to deal with members of the cast in costume, trying to see what the production looks like from the back.

While obviously this practice must be checked – it is very disconcerting for anyone in the back row when someone leans on their chair and on turning round they find themselves face to face with Sweeney Todd – stern measures are useless. The easiest way to clear a member of the cast from the auditorium is simply to say, 'Aren't you due on stage in a minute?' I have seen entire armies flee for the exit at those magic words.

The last and perhaps most important duty of a Coarse house manager is to watch for the director, who will be found snooping round the side aisles muttering 'Oh God' occasionally. Gently lead him away and stop him from trying to climb on stage.

BOX OFFICE. The box-office will be staffed by people congenitally incapable of counting. Either the hall will be over-booked, so twenty people are causing a din at the back trying to get in, or whole chunks of the auditorium will be deserted ('Well, I'm afraid Freda lost that part of the plan'). The only certain thing is that the number of chairs in the hall will bear no relation to the number of squares on the plan.

The greatest menace to a box-office are the actors, who reserve vast chunks of the auditorium for their friends and then fail to sell the tickets, so every night the box-office staff have to deal with several hundred returns from the cast. By some perversity of fate, however, if a show is a sell-out close relations of the cast will besiege the box-office demanding admittance. It is difficult to refuse some one who shouts, 'I have travelled fifty miles from Colchester to see my son in this play and now you won't let me in.'

Sometimes a soft-hearted official gives way and by the time

the relations of all the cast have arrived the hall is a mass of people fighting for chairs.

REFRESHMENT STAFF. The refreshment staff, who appear to be specially trained to make a noise, are under the impression that the interval is the reason for the show. Indeed, often they are not quite certain what is going on in the hall itself. Unfortunately they are usually equally vague about their own department, with the result that it can be taken as a law of Coarse Drama that refreshments are available only ten minutes before the interval and ten minutes after it.

The interval itself is marked by long queues of hopeless, hungry and thirsty people waiting patiently while the refreshment staff try to coax the kettle to boil. This it inevitably does, as the second bell sounds.

PUBLICITY MANAGER. A publicity manager's main task is to deal with the local Press. The only constant factor in this is the photographer, who will always appear punctually an hour before the dress rehearsal starts and demand that all the cast immediately get into costume for the picture. As most of them haven't even arrived by then, he will seize six of the likeliest people, line them up against a half-finished piece of scenery and mow them down with his camera.

The only advantage of this is that it gives the small-part players a chance, since the major characters are never changed in time. The photographer, who invariably has to go and attend another function at once, will then leave hastily without taking any details.

As one who spent many years on provincial newspapers, I know that the routine of photographers cannot be altered and a publicity manager who tries is wasting his time. If even the editor can't do it, the publicity manager cannot hope to succeed.

However, the approach of the critics is less determinable. First there is the reporter without any interest at all. He is easily the best critic to have, as although he will leave at the interval and not return, he will write nothing but fulsome praise. A clever publicity manager will encourage such a critic by writing to the editor and saying how much they appreciated the report (although the reporter will not thank him for this, as it means he has to do the ghastly job again). Have pity for the poor man. After all, he may have seen *The Hostage* fifteen times. Refrain from telling the editor he left at the interval.

A Fleet Street editor confessed to me recently that after watching *A Phoenix Too Frequent* twenty times as a young reporter in North London, he simply wrote the same report each time, merely changing the names of the cast.

If a critic should do this I see no cause for complaint, as long as the original write-up was a good one.

Enthusiastic but ill-informed local reporters provide a problem when they misinterpret things (as with the critic who complained that my production of Pinter's *Silence* 'had too many pauses'). However, he did once ascribe the collapse of Claudius's throne (due to defective construction) as 'symbolic of the fall of a corrupt society', so one should not complain.

This man's worst gaffe was to mistake a woman of sixty-five for her thirty-year-old daughter, thinking she was made up to look old. 'As the grandmother, Sheila Middleton was superb,' he wrote. 'This young woman gave us a brilliant study of decrepit old age, painfully limping about the stage with lined face, bent back and sagging breasts. She really did look sixty-five.'

Some swine cut out the write-up, underlined the bit about sagging breasts and stuck it on the mother's dressing-room mirror.*

The most dangerous critic is the one who knows something about the subject. He, too, will read things into a production that aren't there ('. ... the lesbian undertones in Lady Teazle were not brought out ...') but will sound plausible about it. Flattery will have no effect on him. Writing a rude letter to the editor only pleases him. Free drink makes him irritable. But he won't like being patronized. After an especially vicious piece write and thank him for his 'pleasing little review, which caused much pleasure and amusement among the cast'. Please note, I take no responsibility if the above advice doesn't work.

* Actually, I did it.

This, of course, has not been written from the critic's point of view. The critic could retort that usually there is no one to greet him at the hall, that there is nobody to answer his queries and that attempts to seek information from house officials meet with a vacant stare. Any information vouchsafed is usually inaccurate (it is astonishing how few human beings are capable of stating a simple fact correctly). Not only that, but if he should attempt to mix with the cast afterwards he will certainly be completely ignored.

The critic, however, must remember Law Ten of Coarse Acting: 'All critics are wrong, but those who praise the actors have had a flash of lucidity.'

SECRETARY. Basically there is no such thing as the secretary of an amateur dramatic society because the office changes hands so frequently that any occupant of the secretarial chair is always a temporary passer-by, filling in a few weeks before the committee persuade someone else to take on the post.

The main duties of the secretary are to tone down the committee minutes (censoring such remarks as 'Well, everyone knows you never could act, old boy, you're just jealous . . .') and to compose his letter of resignation ('Regret that after only three weeks in office must reluctantly hand over to someone with more time . . .').

TREASURER. People take on the treasurer's job because they wish to gain revenge on the actors and directors, whom for some reason they envy. As long as this is understood then a lot of friction will be avoided when the treasurer allows a production budget of ten pounds for *Pink Champagne* and spends five hundred pounds on printing an official history of the society.

However, as no one else will understand finance, there is no point in quarrelling with the treasurer. It is impossible to argue with people who use phrases like, 'By writing up the fixed assets we have turned our loss into a profit.' Those of us who have simple minds in which one just adds up what was spent, adds up what was received and subtracts one from the other, are mere pawns.

PLAY SELECTION. This is best done by a small committee. As everyone will disagree with the choice of play it is better that a committee should bear the burden of criticism rather than an individual. Remember the failure of a Coarse Drama production is always blamed on the choice of play, never on the acting.

ORGANIZATION OF THEATRE GROUP. Although in theory most societies are under the control of a committee, one person is usually the inspiration behind every group. Coarse Actors much prefer to avoid responsibility and sit back and criticize with neurotic outbursts at the annual meeting ('Mr Chairman, when are we going to do something about the fact that all our plays are cast by a clique?').

It can be taken for granted that the annual meeting will provide the funniest performance of the year and the only time when most of the speakers will know their lines. But while a Coarse Actor should criticize freely, he must never make the mistake of being elected to anything.

However, a word of warning about the chairman. This post tends to go to an old acting member. At first sight one might think he accepts because of his long service to the society. But it is not so. An old actor who becomes chairman does so in the belief that it will help him get those parts he has been coveting all his vile life, and which up to now have eluded him. Unless watched carefully, within a few months he will have insinuated his own choice of play, insinuated his son as director of it and had himself cast in the best part (probably the juvenile lead).

There is one sure way of dealing with this, however. At the annual meeting at which the chairman is elected a leading member of the society should make a speech of welcome and praise, in which he says quite firmly, 'We all know the sacrifice Harold is making in taking up this arduous post, because it means *he will not be able to act this season . . .*' If that hint does not work, then nothing will.

SOCIAL ORGANIZATION. The social side of a drama group is most important. In fact that is all a great many of the actors and actresses come for. While the formal social events tend to be the acme of dullness, the best are those unrehearsed episodes which arise spontaneously, such as we-all-hate-the-director sessions in the local pub, or the furtive seizing of a pretty ASM in the props cellar.

Unless carefully organized, after-show parties degenerate into boozy mutual congratulation, followed by an orgy of pairing-off and let's-all-go-round-to-Charlie's where the mutual congratulation is turned into a hate session.

The curse of these parties is the people who will insist on doing their piece. Watkins has actually tried to recite *The Highwayman* fifteen times without ever finishing it, but this doesn't matter as no one takes him seriously. The more dangerous sort, however, are those characters, usually new to a society and with an imposing although quite unverifiable reputation, who fix everyone with a baleful eye and announce that they have been persuaded to give an excerpt from an old Welsh verse play, adding modestly that this always used to go down very well when they were with mutter-mutter (nobody quite catches the name, but it sounds impressive).

It is fatal to be polite. They seize on the smallest scattering of applause and do an encore. I knew one chap who went on all night until we seriously considered adopting the old music-hall technique of dragging him off stage with a long stick hooked round his neck.

To deal with a person of this sort greet his well-meant efforts with a chorus of remarks like 'Don't ring us, we'll ring you' and 'We'll let you know, dear'. It sounds cruel, but it is kinder to everyone in the long run.

For some reason people of the type I have described never stay with a society for more than one show. They will next be heard of with some rival society, repeating the same formula.

The best way to make an after-show party go is to perform a vicious skit on the play. This not only gives the cast an opportunity for showing the director what they really think of it, but it gives those not on stage a chance of hooting and jeering. With luck it will also thwart the efforts of any would-be reciters.

10 Festivals and Tours

'The wind was so strong that a stage-hand had to stand behind each wing and hold it up so that it would not topple over towards the audience . . .' CONSTANTIN STANISLAVSKI

Alarming experience at festivals – mystery of the missing flats – appeal to Tamworth Co-operative Society – when they tried to hang Askew – Unpleasantness in one of Her Majesty's prisons – lost in a school – the Unpleasantness over *Tannhäuser*

A Coarse Actor is at his best on tour or at a festival – when playing away from home, so to speak. A strange stage, a strange audience, perhaps even a strange part of the country, offer great opportunities for him. No Coarse Actor should ever neglect the opportunity of appearing in a festival, if only for the pleasure of looking back on an unpleasant experience and thinking how good it is that the event is over.

Festival troubles begin with transport. It is the Eleventh Law of Coarse Drama that the properties, scenery and costumes will never arrive intact (a sub-section of the law states that the cast are quite likely not to arrive intact, either).

I would give five pounds to know what happened to the scenery for our production of *Black Comedy*. The stage manager swears that it was carefully checked and loaded on to our van, yet when the vehicle arrived two flats were missing. The van doors were still locked. Who would want to steal two flats?

Even if you are lucky enough to have scenery the costumes will not all be there. Few feelings in life equal the pang of horror that goes through an actor when the skip has been emptied and his trousers still have not been found. This, of course, can make for some interesting performances. When my friend Askew's entire costume vanished he wrapped himself in two tablecloths and played the part as a Scotsman. In view of the fact that he was supposed to be portraying the Duke of Orleans he came in for some criticism by the adjudicator, but the main thing is that the show went on.

The only way to be safe is take your own costume, or, better still, wear it.

Be careful of the properties and scenery. In the confusion, as rival teams of stage-hands jostle with each other, things can go astray. We once came away with a completely worthless door, labelled 'Tamworth Co-operative Society Drama Group', in exchange for a marvellous flat which had been painted for us by the designer at the local rep.

As regards acting in a festival, remember that the audience are not merely different from at home but actively hostile. Apart from your own tiny clique it will consist entirely of the friends and relatives of other competing societies, so don't think you're going to get away with any of those characteristic bits of business that go down so well at home. Be prepared to act in stony silence, broken only by the strained and polite laughter of the local mayor, who feels he must make an effort.

To this must be added the further disadvantage that the stage is strange and that the festival stage manager is a tame saboteur in league with a rival group. I was once just about to make an entrance when one of these gentlemen seized my arm and pulled me away, saying, 'You can't stand here, we've got to store a flat in this hole.'

I forced my way on stage after a great struggle, protesting and shaking my fist to such an effect that the adjudicator later complimented me on my entrance. The only trouble came when I tried to go off and found the exit blocked with someone else's set.

The adjudication should not be taken too much to heart if it is critical. If it is full of praise, of course, then take it seriously. Remember that the adjudicator would not be reduced to doing the job if he could earn money any other way in the Theatre. Actually most adjudicators are terribly nice people, even the one who said he never heard a word I spoke. I am genuinely prepared to believe he was deaf.

The primary job of a director at a festival is to keep his cast
off the beer. Coarse Actors go berserk away from home. As
soon as they pile out of their cars, instead of examining the
dressing-rooms, getting the pitch of the hall and so on, they
will move into the centre of the road, sniff the air for a
moment and then march into the nearest boozer.

If left there they will come back in half an hour, laughing
foolishly, slurring their words, and with bottles of light ale
sticking from their pockets. Once that happens it is as well to
write off the whole production, although the cast will doubtless have a wonderful time.

After the production is a different matter. Leave one non-
drinker behind to hear the adjudication and to receive the
cup (if any) and immediately retire to the nearest bar.

In the old Coventry Festival the Northampton team went
straight across the road into the Union Arms and immediately
became involved in a long argument about rugby with some
local people. By some extraordinary error we won the cup
and they had to send messengers to search the district for us.
We all climbed beerily on to the stage over the orchestra
stalls, and when the mayor handed over the cup our director
promptly dropped it, while we all cheered and blinked
drunkenly at the audience, which did not create a very good
impression. All this could have been avoided if we had left
someone behind.

TOURS. While the same difficulties and pleasures apply to
these, there is the added advantage that the show, being
non-competitive, usually has the audience on the side of the
actors. The chance has now gone, fortunately, for the greatest
touring experience of all time, the wartime ENSA troupe, a
case in which I think it could definitely be said that the
audience were not on the side of the actors.

My friend Askew claims that after a show in North Africa,
during which he did a comic turn satirizing the Australian
Army, he came out of the dressing-tent to find five Australians
waiting for him with a rope.

Whatever troubles may beset a Coarse tour, the actor
should be thankful that he has not the difficulties that used to
face the ENSA artistes, desperately making bad jokes about

the shortage of beer to three thousand bored and recalcitrant soldiery, only a quarter of whom could hear what was being said.

It is, however, still possible to play to service audiences, although here a Coarse Actor must decide whether the advantages of free drinks in the officers' mess outweigh the shuffling and chattering that will accompany a presentation of Molière to the 25 Field Ammunition Dump. For those Coarse Actors who never reached commissioned rank there is the added difficulty that old army habits never really die, and they will find themselves standing to attention and cringing when the mess corporal hands them a gin.

For some reason directors always seem to pick unsuitable plays for service audiences, doubtless fired with missionary zeal to take culture to the lads. Unfortunately actors are persistently associated in the military mind with effeminacy, and any eighteenth-century bowing and fluttering will bring a howl of high-pitched mocking voices, combined with rough jests which I will not repeat here. My advice is simply not to take part in anything with the slightest suspicion of grace and elegance. It will be completely misinterpreted.

In fact treat all tours with suspicion. I once allowed myself to be mixed up in a murder play which they took to a prison, of all places. I was playing a policeman. I have been greeted by some strange noises in my time but never has my entrance been heralded by anything like the sound that came as I walked on stage in the gaol recreation room. I very nearly walked straight off again. Every time I opened my mouth to speak there was a near riot.

The back-stage staff, who were mostly prisoners, were very decent about it and explained that the lads were a little upset because a mass-break-out had been foiled the day before and the ring-leaders were languishing in solitary. I told the governor that I thought the prisoner who was working the lights seemed an awfully pleasant sort of man, and the governor said he had recently stabbed someone with a dinner knife, being given to uncontrollable fits of violence.

'You were lucky he didn't have a go at you when he saw your copper's uniform,' he added jovially.

Despite all this, I would prefer to act in a prison than in a school. Give me the honest criminal any day in preference to children.

An audience of children is simply a collection of malevolent minds waiting for an excuse to make a noise. Unfortunately Coarse Acting offers them plenty of opportunity for this. Where an adult audience will merely stir uncomfortably at a prompt, an audience of children will say loudly, 'He's forgotten his lines, he can't remember what he's got to say next, he'll have to ask that lady peering round the edge of the scenery . . .' It's almost impossible to stand up to that sort of thing.

It is dangerous to act to children in the round, or without the protection of a solid proscenium arch. Even in normal conditions things are bad enough, what with the senior boys smoking in the back row and making amorous experiments with the senior girls, and the youngsters talking and chewing sweets in front, but without the proscenium the wretches have an opportunity to get at the actor physically.

During an apron-stage production of *St Joan* I watched with horror as a little infant sitting at the side of the apron got up and caught hold of the butt end of somebody's spear. There was a little tug-of-war which only ended when the distraught actor jabbed the spear violently backwards into the child's ribs.

Afterwards the child's mother wrote to the director and complained her son had a great weal on his ribs, but the director had had enough by then and replied his only regret was that it wasn't the child's head.

Sometimes children will even talk to the actors. It is a little disconcerting when a tiny hand tugs at one's cloak and a voice pipes up, 'Mister, do you know there's a hole in your sock?'

It is fatal to ignore the voice, because the questioner becomes even more persistent until he is answered. And it is equally fatal to engage the child in conversation, because the conversation never finishes.

I am afraid there is only one thing to do to child conversationalists. Say two magic words. I will not repeat them here, but I do assure readers that the effects are instantaneous and in the ensuing silence it may be possible to work over to the other side of the stage.

Another difficulty of touring is that the stage is often improvised in a place not normally used for dramatic performances, and one is frequently playing at floor level, as in a hospital ward or a school gymnasium.

It was this which led to the Unpleasantness at Perivale, where as Sir Lucius O'Trigger I swept superbly off a school stage with the intention of returning from the other side two minutes later. I walked out of the tiny wings and through a door, turned right, and went through another door which should have led to a passage at right angles to the stage.

I was rather surprised to find myself in a classroom where evening students were studying life drawing. After a moment's embarrassment I retired and took the next door on the right, which turned out to be the boiler house. The man stoking the furnace summed up the situation neatly when he said: 'Ah mate, you're in the wrong room. You want the next door but two down the corridor.'

By this time I was becoming rather worried. I ran to the door he indicated. It was a Scottish dancing class. I honestly think I would still be floating round that wretched school if I hadn't heard laughter in the distance. I knew that sound. It was the noise made by a group of children when an actor fails to appear. Guided by the noise, which was increasing in intensity, I ran through a door into the playground and saw the lights of the hall. It was no time for niceties. I simply pulled open an emergency exit at the back and dashed in, spattered with rain. The kids loved it.

Occasionally the unexpected happens on tour and one is embarrassed by the lavishness of the stage. Some years ago Askew and I played in an amateur production of *Twelfth Night* which toured Germany and Austria. We took with us a ludicrous assembly of cheap wood and nuts and bolts, which was our all-purpose 'set'. When erected it formed a pathetic square bower, rather like a small public convenience, and when dismantled it fell apart into a collection of pieces which would never fit the bag in which they were carried.

We duly arrived at the Opera House in Klagenfurt, Austria. The stage of this is rather formidable, about the size of Wembley Stadium. We had a matinée for local schools, sandwiched between a performance by a professional German company of *Die Walküre* the previous night and *Tannhäuser* the same evening.

The stage manager and the director arrived with our pathetic bag of little sticks and dumped it on the stage. It looked rather lonely. A troop of twenty stage-hands appeared, headed by Herr Stage Direktor.

'Please,' he enquired, 'you wish us to erect your set immediately?'

'Good heavens, no,' said our director, who was a rather fussy man. 'We couldn't trust you with a set like this. I'm the only person who knows how to put it together, old boy. Unless you do it in a certain order you get a bit left over at the end.'

Herr Direktor looked put out.

'It is good,' he said, with an expression which indicated that it wasn't, and he marched away his stage staff.

The performance went on and ended. Immediately the ninety-foot curtain had fallen Herr Direktor marched on stage.

'Please,' he said, 'will you have the goodness to remove your scenery as we wish immediately to set *Tannhäuser* for the performance in an hour's time.'

Our director became flustered.

'I'm doing it as fast as I can,' he said stiffly. 'You must remember that unless it's done in a certain way we can't pack it.'

Herr Direktor made a strange Teutonic sign. Twenty men emerged from the shadows.

Next moment our little pavilion was whirling round on the revolve while the director, who was off the revolving section, chased after it. As he did so, *Tannhäuser* descended from the flies, nearly braining him. He finally caught up with our set after it had travelled about a hundred yards, but before he could start work they began to set *Valküre* all round it.

It was two hours before the director crept out into the street, dragging his little canvas bag of bits. Next day, when we arrived in Vienna, we found a piece of wood was missing. We wrote to Herr Direktor, but he never returned it.

Some companies take shows on tour to hospitals. This does guarantee a passive audience, most of them too numbed by weeks in bed to make any reaction at all, although domestic disturbances, such as faint cries for a bedpan, can be disturbing during a performance.

Not that I see why sick or elderly people should have Coarse Acting inflicted on them without any choice in the matter. One of the great Drama fallacies is that people who are old or ill have lost their critical faculties and are grateful to have any sort of tripe served up.

I shall not easily forget chairing an Old Time Music Hall at a cripples' centre, at which the audience showed their opinion by starting to wheel their invalid chairs all over the hall to talk to their friends. Some of them were kind enough to wave a stick at me and shout 'Don't mind us – just carry on' as they whizzed past. Another offered me a cup of tea in the middle of my best funny story.

I don't blame them a bit. No one has a right to impose a bad amateur dramatic show on the helpless.

The Edinburgh Festival is one of the great experiences of touring, despite that peculiar breed of Edinburgh janitors (or servitors as they are called) who take over the production of the play themselves.

'Ye can no have that nude scene in this hall' they say firmly. 'The lassie must clothe her wee loins . . .' Or else it's, 'Ye can rehearse for one hour exactly and then Ah'm turnin' oot the lights as it's mah night off.'

Edinburgh provided me with a macabre stage experience when we took *The Coarse Acting Show* there for the first time. We celebrated a successful first night with a party and at 3 a.m. we were demonstrating golf strokes when one of the cast got hit on the head by a backswing which knocked him unconscious and cut his head badly.

At 4.30 that morning I might have been seen walking up and down the casualty department of Edinburgh Royal Infirmary trying to learn the injured man's lines. The first thing he heard on recovering consciousness was me repeating his lines the other side of the screen, and he cried out feebly, 'Don't let Mike play my part . . . I'll do it somehow.''

An example of how the threat of losing a part will spur a Coarse Actor to any lengths. Yes, he did manage to totter on stage that evening with nine stitches in his face.

11

'Tis Pity She's the Merry Wife of Henry VI (Part One)

Being a risible Elizabethan tragi-comedy-history, dedicated to whomever happens to be in power at the present, and especially written for the amateur stage with the intention of affording opportunities for a Coarse Actor to play seven different parts, all of increasing moronity.

ACT ONE

SCENE ONE: *A room in the castle of St Albans. Flourish. Enter hautboys. Enter King with Darlington, Doncaster, Retford, Grantham, Newark, Peterborough, Welwyn, Hitchin and their trains. Enter Coarse Actor carrying flagon of wine. While they are all dressed in the usual Shakespearean odds-and-ends the Coarse Actor stands out by reason of his stock small part costume, the crowning glory of which is an obscene pair of old tights whose crutch is somewhere around his knees. The procession goes round and round meaninglessly. Exeunt.*

SCENE TWO: *Another part of St Albans. Flourish. Enter King with lords and attendants as before, minus cupbearer.*

KING: My Lord of Darlington, what news from Scotland?

DARLINGTON: My liege, there is even at this moment an emissary arrived from Ross.

There is a long pause.

DARLINGTON (*savagely*): My liege, there is *even at this moment* an emissary arrived from Ross.

The Coarse Actor arrives with a kilt tied hastily over his tights.

KING: Thy panting breathe betrays thy haste. I like it not.
    Say, tell me what thy tidings are.

CA: My liege –

KING: Know thou, thou scurvy messenger, that we
    Have fifteen nights now watched Orion turn
    His vasty arc in yon benighted sky
    And fifteen times have heard bad news from Ross.
    What can'st thou bring to ease our royal burden?

CA (*in atrocious Scottish accent*): My liege, I bring thee nothing
    but defiance,
    The rebel host, consuming all before it, doth already –

> *The King gives a growl of fury and rises and picks up the
> messenger by the equivalent of his lapels. He shakes him savagely
> and then flings him into the footlights in an immense cloud of dust
> which has arisen from his costume. He lies grovelling.*

KING: Thou naughty messenger!
    These tidings that thou bringst mislike us well.
    And for the evil news that thou hast brought
    I'll have thee flogged throughout the town tonight,
    Thus shalt thou know defiance is not made
    So easily against our royal person.
    Go drag him hence and beat him mightily.

CA: My liege, I – WHURP . . . .

> (*He is dragged out with unnecessary force.*)

KING: Go, Darlington, and cousin Grantham too.
    Get thee ten thousand men and meet me here
    Tomorrow. Let all bend unto his task
    Until the rebels do for mercy ask.

> *His voice rises to an Olivier-type shriek. His crown falls off.*
>
> *Exeunt.*

SCENE THREE: *Another room in the castle at St Albans. Enter the
Queen, with fifteen attendants, one of whom is the Coarse Actor who
has got rid of his kilt but probably retains vestiges of his Scottish
costume elsewhere. He is carrying a property lute with slack strings
made of string. He plays this furiously. Suddenly, with a screech, the*

noise of a lute bursts forth at deafening amplification just as he stops playing. He starts again hurriedly. The lute sound stops suddenly with a noise suggesting a tape recorder in pain. The Coarse Actor carries on vigorously.

QUEEN: Oh woe! Alack the day!
ALL: Oh woe! Alack the day! Ruhubarb! Woe the day! Alack the woe! Rhubarb! etc.

> *Exeunt for no reason at all, Queen weeping. Last out is the Coarse Actor who has now got his hand firmly trapped in the strings of the lute.*

ACT TWO

SCENE ONE: *A street in St Albans. A certain vile noise is heard. Enter First Clown and Coarse Actor as Assistant Clown or all-purpose Shakespearean stooge. He is walking with a strange gait that suggests an internal injury, because he thinks this is how clowns should walk.*

FIRST CLOWN: By the Mass thou look'st as sad as a quondam neat's tongue dried at Blackfriars, the one the French tailor could not stomach.
CA: Aye, marry and amen.

> *They pause, because the director has told them this is funny. It is, however, received in silence, except for the rustle of programmes as the audience look to see if this pair are supposed to be comics.*

FIRST CLOWN: I will cheer thee with some merry jests. Tell me, good neighbour Clodpony, why is a codpiece like a candle-maker?
CA: Nay, I know not.
FIRST CLOWN: Thou makest light of the jest; and doth not a candlemaker make light also? Therefore thou art a very candlemaker indeed. Ergo, thou art a codpiece.

> *The CA bursts into unconvincing and exaggerated laughter.*

CA: An were I a codpiece I should know where to hide my light.

> *They fall about with simulated mirth.*

FIRST CLOWN: Prithee, dost think the King will defeat the rebels?

CA: Aye, he were no King otherwise.

FIRST CLOWN: That were a royal remark. An were the King no King he would be a rebel indeed. (*He pauses for a laugh which never comes*) But come old Clodpony, answer me this. What is it that hath a horn and hath not a horn?

He places his fingers on his forehead in the traditional horn sign.

CA: God's sonties, but I know not.

FIRST CLOWN: Stir thy wits.

CA: Alas, I have none.

FIRST CLOWN: Why, the answer is: a cuckold when Michaelmas falls on a Thursday.

CA: But why on Thursday?

FIRST CLOWN: Mass, I know not.

CA: No more I prithee, lest I injure myself with laughing at the subtlety of thy jests.

He rocks with immoderate laughter which is interrupted by the First Clown savagely beating him with his bladder.

FIRST CLOWN: But let's away. We must to St Albans to see the King.

Both exit, gibbering and mowing.
There is the sound of people leaving the audience.

SCENE TWO: *The rebel camp near St Albans. Enter Wolverton, Bletchley, Blisworth, Rugby, Nuneaton, Stafford and Crewe, muttering.*

BLETCHLEY: Therefore, brothers, unto our several tasks.
And ere yon Phoebus thrice five times has passed
Over this wrinkled orb we call the earth
The King shall know the mettle of our minds.

BLISWORTH: Aye, and perchance the metal of our swords.

Everyone falls about with mirth.

BLETCHLEY: Why, that's my brother Blisworth. I do know the sharpness of thy wit and relish thee the more withal.

NUNEATON: The King will not relish us, my lord.

STAFFORD: He will find us too hot for his relish.
BLISWORTH: Too hot? Nay then we shall pepper him.

There is a positive explosion of mirth at this hilarious exchange.

BLETCHLEY: Where's Wolverton?
BLISWORTH: Somewhere in Buckinghamshire.
BLETCHLEY: Enough, coz. Be not a spendthrift with thy jests lest haply some may return to thee. Is Wolverton here?

There is a heaving at the back of the throng and the Coarse Actor bursts on-stage, having made several unavailing efforts to burst through previously. He has now put on a lord's surcoat but cannot hide the obscene tights which are his trademark. He still wears the lute.

CA: Here, my lord.
BLETCHLEY: Then hie thee to St Albans. Carry our defiance to the King.
CA: I will with upmost speed, my lord.

Exeunt.

ACT THREE

SCENE ONE: *The King's camp. A tucket sounds.*

KING: Who is this man with looks so wild who gurdily approaches us?

Enter CA.

CA: My liege I bring letters from Bletchley.
KING: The very name is hideous in mine ears!
    Vile Bletchley! Perfidious, evil man!
    I'll none of them. And thou return to him
    And tell him so, thou wart.

During the last two lines he delivers the now-familiar assault upon the Coarse Actor, hurling him savagely to the ground. The Coarse Actor limps off.

A LORD: What now, my liege?
KING: To arms, that's all a man can do.

ALL: Aye, to arms, it's all a man can do.
KING: If fate should choose we are to die today . . .
ALL: Aye, today, fate, choose etc.
KING: Let's die at least with armour on our backs.
ALL: Aye, with armour, on our backs, at least . . .
KING: Let not the sun shine more
    If St Albans in rebel hands is sure.
ALL: St Albans, in rebel hands, sure, rhubarb . . .

> *The King charges off followed by the army, some of whom trip over their spears.*

SCENE TWO: *Part of the battle. The main battle is going on in the dressing-room where the Coarse Actor has wiped off his earlier make-up and exchanged it for a scrofulous beard, as he is now on the King's side (temporarily).Over his tights he has pulled knitted chainmail trousers of thick string, which have split up the back in a rather obscene fashion. He reaches the wings with some difficulty, as an army is trying to rush off stage, and finds he has forgotten his sword. He hopefully seizes a passing weapon and runs on stage with it.*

BLETCHLEY: Our cause doth prosper well.
    I'll make up to my brother Wolverton.
CA: Hold, rebel.
BLETCHLEY: Who art thou?
CA: I am Sir John Thomas Erpingham-Blunt.
BLETCHLEY: Then defend thyself.

> *They fight. This consists of continually crossing swords and grunting. Occasionally they lock hilts and in one daring move Bletchley beats at the CA's shield. Suddenly the CA holds out his left arm, Bletchley passes his sword under the armpit and the CA drops, gurgling horribly.*

CA: Oh, I die.

> *He remembers to expire behind a piece of scenery, crawls off, changes shields and returns at once.*

BLETCHLEY: Then farewell, good Sir Thomas. I'll to my brother Stafford.

> *Enter Darlington.*

DARLINGTON: The King doth labour mightily.
　　　　　　　I'll rest me here and see what I can see.

Enter Coarse Actor after changing his shield.

CA: Stand!
DARLINGTON: Thou rebel dog, I'll teach thee tell me stand.
　Sayst stand dost thou? Then stand upon thy stand or I'll
　unstand thee.

He waves his sword vaguely in the air.

CA: Oh, I am dust.

　He dies.

　*Nevertheless he manages to crawl off stage, where, flinging a
　cloak over his armour, he ties himself up with rope and waits to be
　dragged on stage as a rebel prisoner. Unfortunately no one
　appears to do this, so when the cue comes he slinks on by himself,
　holding the rope out horizontally in front of him to indicate he is
　being led.*

KING (*recovering from his surprise*): What surly men are
　these?
NEWARK: The rebel prisoners, my liege.
KING: Their very sight offends me. I will none
　Of them. Go hang them all with utmost speed
　About St Albans market square. Cut off
　Their rebellious noses on the way
　And beat their naughty persons mightily.

　　　Exit Coarse Actor being beaten.

KING: News have we that the weasel French, consumed
　With envy at our royal success is e'en
　Against now in arms. Thus meet it is
　That we with speediness do take our leave.
　The dead in pious clay we'll cover
　And then immediately proceed to Dover.
ALL: On toward Dover ho!

　　*Exeunt in procession. Just as they are leaving, the CA, who has
　　changed again, enters at the tail of the queue.*

CA: On toward Dover, ho!

> *He passes into the wings where he immediately starts to collect the tea money.*

THE END

* Application to perform *'Tis Pity She's The Merry Wife* . . . should be made to Curtis Brown Ltd., 1, Craven Hill, London W2 3EW. Some material has since been incorporated in *Four Plays for Coarse Actors* (published by Samuel French) and *The Coarse Acting Show 2*, and these might provide more suitable acting versions. Anyone foolish enough to want to run a Coarse Acting Competition can obtain permission and the rules from Curtis Brown, together with several hundred words of advice from myself.

Epilogue

Spoken by the Author

The Critic sitting in his slippered ease
Says we who please to write must write to please.
(Though now it's easier to fill the belly
By being rude to people on the telly.
And fellows with the wit of a capillary
Prosper by putting persons in the pillory.)

I'll none of this; and should my book offend
(Especially in reference to my friends)
I penitent will always be: I swear it,
But if the cap fits, mate, then bloomin' wear it.